MEN ON MOO

"ONE SMALL STEP FOR MA
ONE GIANT LEAP FOR MANK

First Family Saves Crew
from 'Kra-Torr'

A Powde
Is Clos

NIXON REJECTS
COMMITTE SUB

Bombing of Demilitarised
Zone in Vietnam Continues

TAPES AND PAPERS

FP SHAKEN UP

w Accusations fly
egarding Ties to
'Shadow Lords'

2

KURT BUSIEK
writer

BRENT ERIC ANDERSON
artist

ALEX SINCLAIR
colors

ALEX ROSS
covers

JG ROSHELL & COMICRAFT
lettering & design

BUSIEK, ANDERSON & ROSS
cultural historians

ASTRO CITY: THE DARK AGE

1: BROTHERS & OTHER STRANGERS

ANN HUNTINGTON BUSIEK
Managing Editor

RICHARD STARKINGS
Art Director

TERRI CUNNINGHAM
VP—Managing Editor

ALISON GILL
VP—Manufacturing

DAVID HYDE
VP—Publicity

HANK KANALZ
VP—General Manager,
WildStorm

PAULA LOWITT
Senior VP—Business & Legal
Affairs

MARYELLEN MCLAUGHLIN
VP—Advertising & Custom
Publishing

GREGORY NOVECK
Senior VP—Creative Affairs

SUE POHJA
VP—Book Trade Sales

STEVE ROTTERDAM
Senior VP—Sales & Marketing

CHERYL RUBIN
Senior VP—Brand Management

JEFF TROJAN
VP—Business Development,
DC Direct

BOB WAYNE
VP—Sales

JIM LEE
Editorial Director

JOHN NEE
Senior VP—Business
Development

BEN ABERNATHY
Editor

KRISTY QUINN
Assistant Editor

ED ROEDER
Art Director

PAUL LEVITZ
President & Publisher

GEORG BREWER
VP—Design & DC Direct Creative

RICHARD BRUNING
Senior VP—Creative Director

PATRICK CALDON
Executive VP—Finance &
Operations

CHRIS CARAMALIS
VP—Finance

JOHN CUNNINGHAM
VP—Marketing

Originally Published in ASTRO CITY/ARROWSMITH #1, ASTRO CITY: THE DARK AGE BOOK ONE #1-4 and ASTRO CITY: THE DARK AGE BOOK TWO #1-4.

ASTRO CITY: THE DARK AGE 1: BROTHERS AND OTHER STRANGERS. Published by WildStorm Productions. 888 Prospect St. #240, La Jolla, CA 92037. Cover, introduction, sketches and compilation Copyright © 2008 Juke Box Productions. All Rights Reserved. Astro City, its logos, symbols, prominent characters featured in this issue and the distinctive likenesses thereof are trademarks of Juke Box Productions.

WildStorm and logo are trademarks of DC Comics. Any similarity to institutions or persons living or dead is unintentional and purely coincidental. Printed on recyclable paper. WildStorm does not read or accept unsolicited submissions of ideas, stories or artwork. Printed in Canada.

DC Comics, a Warner Bros. Entertainment Company.

Hardcover ISBN 978-1-4012-1868-3 · Softcover ISBN 978-1-4012-2077-8

DC BOOKS BY THE SAME CREATORS:

ASTRO CITY: LIFE IN THE BIG CITY
ASTRO CITY: CONFESSION
ASTRO CITY: FAMILY ALBUM
ASTRO CITY: THE TARNISHED ANGEL
ASTRO CITY: LOCAL HEROES

BY KURT BUSIEK

AQUAMAN: ONCE AND FUTURE
(with Butch Guice)

ARROWSMITH: SO SMART IN THEIR FINE UNIFORMS (with Carlos Pacheco)

JLA/AVENGERS (with George Pérez)

JLA: SYNDICATE RULES (with Ron Garney)

SUPERMAN: BACK IN ACTION
(with Fabian Nicieza & Pete Woods)

SUPERMAN: CAMELOT FALLS vol. 1-2
(with Carlos Pacheco)

SUPERMAN: REDEMPTION
(with Fabian Nicieza)

SUPERMAN: SECRET IDENTITY
(with Stuart Immonen)

SUPERMAN: 3-2-1-ACTION
(with Brad Walker)

SUPERMAN: UP, UP AND AWAY
(with Geoff Johns & Pete Woods)

THE WIZARD'S TALE (with David Wenzel)

BY BRENT ANDERSON

LEGACY: THE LAST WILL & TESTAMENT OF HAL JORDAN (with Joe Kelly)

BY ALEX ROSS

BATMAN: WAR ON CRIME (with Paul Dini)

JLA: LIBERTY AND JUSTICE (with Paul Dini)

JUSTICE vol. 1-3
(with Jim Krueger & Doug Braithwaite)

KINGDOM COME (with Mark Waid)

MYTHOLOGY: THE DC COMICS ART OF ALEX ROSS

SHAZAM: POWER OF HOPE (with Paul Dini)

SUPERMAN: PEACE ON EARTH (with Paul Dini)

UNCLE SAM (with Steve Darnall)

WONDER WOMAN: SPIRIT OF TRUTH
(with Paul Dini)

DEDICATIONS

For Dave, Ted, Steve, Randall and Guy,
my brothers-in-law....and one out-law...
— Kurt

For Alfredo Alcala, Dave Cockrum,
Steve Gerber, Jim Mooney and
Marshall Rogers. Masters of the
Universe, one and all.
— Brent

For Huggy Bear, without whom
this book would not exist.
— Alex

NIXON RESIGNS

URGES 'TIME OF HEALING'

CONTENTS

I am one lucky bastard.

No, I'm not talking about my lovely wife and two equally lovely daughters (they're what make me one lucky S.O.B. — but that's the intro of a different book). I'm one lucky bastard because I'm a lifelong comic book fan who gets paid to write comic books. And for guys (in the gender-neutral sense) like me there are four types of comic books: books you don't read; books you do read; books you write; and books you wish you wrote.

Guess which category *Astro City* falls into?

If you answered, "None of the Above," you're correct. For so many reasons, *Astro City* belongs in a category — nay, a *class* — by itself: Books you wish you'd *created*. Reading an issue of *Astro City* makes me sick with envy for Kurt Busiek's fertile imagination, encyclopedic knowledge of all things comic book, and inventiveness to combine the two into a sprawling epic that spans decades.

Now if you've read any of the previous *Astro City* stories, you might be tempted to write off the details and characters therein as random — little wisps of names and dates that were thrown in to add spice to the sauce, but not necessarily to promise some larger, specific story, not to suggest a grand plan.

Not to presage a sixteen-issue epic like *The Dark Age*.

You'd be justified in thinking that there wasn't something larger at work because, like a gifted prestidigitator, Mr. Busiek is employing sleight of hand to distract you from the larger saga he's laying the foundation for right beneath your feet and under your nose. The means of distraction he's using is a little thing we writer-types like to call "character."

In *Astro City*, the triumphs of good over evil, the collisions of worlds and the never-ending battles take a back seat to the people living, loving, working and sometimes dying in the shadows of such pivotal moments. Unlike other comics, where the clash of inter-dimensional civilizations would get a 12-issue maxi-series company-wide crossover, *Astro City* might — *might* — devote a panel to it. (Though you can be damn certain that Mr. Busiek has mapped out every plot twist and detail of the conflagration.)

Instead, the story would focus on the D-list villain looking to "make the big time" by taking advantage of the anarchy resulting from said inter-dimensional warfare. Or the hero who, faced with her own mortality in the aftermath of the inter-dimensional crisis, tries to make amends with her estranged sidekick. This is the brilliance of *Astro City*: in a book dealing with all forms of super-humanity, Mr. Busiek never loses sight of the fact that stories should be about *humanity*. In other words, heroes (and, yes, villains) are people, too.

Which is not to say that all of *Astro City*'s stories are concerned with the super-powered. Some of the best, in fact, have focused on very ordinary people, or "Average Joes" as the denizens of Astro City might be wont to call themselves. Case in point: *The Dark Age*, the first half of which you hold in your hand. It's fitting that for this, the most sweeping and ambitious of all of *Astro City*'s stories to date, Mr. Busiek would choose two very normal, all-too-human protagonists through which to weave his story: Charles and Royal Williams. I don't want to ruin your enjoyment of the story of the Williams brothers by telling you their tale here. Suffice it to say, it could stand on its own as a heartfelt drama of fraternal conflict and unrequited emotions — even if their lives didn't occasionally intersect with cosmic crises and crime syndicates.

But, like I said, that's par for the course when we're talking about *Astro City*.

What makes *The Dark Age* stand apart from earlier *Astro City* stories is that without ever losing the focus on character that makes this series so special, we also start to get a clearer picture of the grand epic I keep alluding to.

When you first read *Astro City* Volume 2, Number One, did you wonder what the inscription on the Silver Agent's tomb meant? For that matter, did you wonder how he died in the first place? Well, wonder no more. Were you curious how Rex joined the First Family? You soon won't be. How did the Deacon rise to the top of the criminal food chain? Find out here. (Hint: Royal Williams is to blame, at least partially.) Why did Alex Ross bother designing a costume for a hero (the Street Angel) who only showed up in two panels previously? Because Mr. Busiek's plan is so thorough he knew that S.A. (as his friends know him) would loom large in the *Dark Age* epic.

And there are probably a hundred more (at least) little seeds that were planted in previous issues of *Astro City* that sprout in *The Dark Age*, but I wasn't too smart to notice them. You see, I'm not nearly as smart a person, or as clever a writer, as Mr. Busiek. Nevertheless, he asked me to write this introduction.

Like I said, I'm one lucky bastard.

And if this book is your first exposure to *Astro City*, so are you.

Marc Guggenheim
March 11, 2008
Los Angeles, California

MARC GUGGENHEIM'S FIRST CLAIM TO FAME WAS COLORING THE SHORT STORY "ABSOLUTE ZERO" IN *MARVEL COMICS PRESENTS* #74. BUT HE WENT ON TO BIGGER AND BETTER THINGS—INCLUDING A LAW DEGREE AND WRITING CREDITS ON SUCH TV SERIES AS *THE PRACTICE, LAW & ORDER, JACK & BOBBY, CSI: MIAMI, BROTHERS & SISTERS* AND OTHERS—AND IS ALSO THE CO-CREATOR OF THE TV SERIES *ELI STONE*. COMICS NEVER QUITE LET GO, HOWEVER, AND SINCE WRITING AN *AQUAMAN* FILL-IN IN 2005, HE'S WORKED ON SUCH SERIES AS *THE FLASH, WOLVERINE, AMAZING SPIDER-MAN* AND HIS NEW *YOUNG X-MEN* SERIES. THESE DAYS, HE DIVIDES HIS TIME BETWEEN HOLLYWOOD, THE MARVEL UNIVERSE AND HIS CREATOR-OWNED SERIES *RESURRECTION*, AT ONI PRESS.

THE DARK AGE **PRELUDE**

IT WAS BAKERVILLE, IN *1959.*

I DON'T THINK EITHER OF US ARE *EVER* GONNA FORGET THAT DAY.

APPLES 15¢ POUND

HEY!

HEY, *KID!* YOU *COME BACK!* I *KNOW* YOU -- I *KNOW* YOUR POP!

HA HA HA HA!

CHARLES! YOU CAN'T --

CHARLES, THAT WAS *STEALING!* IF *POPPA* FINDS OUT --

AW, WHAT'S HE GONNA *DO?* OL' MAN EVANS TELLS POPPA, I JUST SAY IT WASN'T ME, IT WAS SOME *OTHER* KID.

YOU WANT A --

CHOOM WRAM KOMM

HUH? WHAT'S --

PEOPLE CALLED IT A TIME THE *WORLD* CHANGED. WE DIDN'T KNOW ANYTHING ABOUT THAT.

ALL WE KNEW *THAT* DAY --

-- WAS THAT STUFF WE'D NORMALLY HEAR MOMMA AND POPPA TALK ABOUT OVER *DINNER* -- STUFF IN THE *NEWSPAPER* --

-- THERE IT *WAS*, RIGHT THERE.

THEY CALLED THEMSELVES *HONOR GUARD*. THE *SILVER AGENT*, *LEOPARDMAN*, *STARWOMAN*, AND THE REST. THEY'D ONLY JUST BECOME A TEAM.

THEY'D FOUGHT *KROSETH THE INVADER*, *COMMISSAR HAMMER* AND THE *STEEL SICKLE*, THE *BEASTMEN*...

THIS WAS PART OF THEIR FIRST BIG CLASH WITH *PYRAMID*, AFTER PYRAMID TRIED TO KIDNAP THE *MERCURY ASTRONAUTS*.

THEY SAY IT WAS THE START OF *SOMETHING NEW* -- THE SECOND BIG WAVE OF HEROES, THE DAWN OF THE SIXTIES, THE BIRTH OF THE SPACE AGE, WHATEVER. AND I GUESS IT *WAS*.

Seink
Bran
Coffee

IT'S JUST NOT SOMETHING YOU EXPECT TO SEE HAPPEN IN *FRONT* OF YOU. NOT IN BAKERVILLE, ANYWAY. NOT IN 1959.

On MULBERRY STREET
A PRELUDE

16

THE *LOOK* IN POPPA'S EYES, WHEN WE TOLD HIM ... I ONLY SAW IT *ONCE* BEFORE, WHEN ROYAL GOT ALL A's ON A REPORT CARD.

WELL, I'LL BE. YOU BOYS *REALLY* DID THAT? *NO FOOLIN'?*

I'VE BEEN HEARING ABOUT ALL THE FIGHTIN' ON THE *RADIO,* BUT... YOU AND THE *BLACK BADGE,* HUH?

I DON'T *KNOW,* LLOYD. I DON'T LIKE THE IDEA OF CHARLES AND ROYAL *OUT THERE* IF THAT SORT OF THING IS HAPPENING. THEY COULD HAVE BEEN --

TOSH, WILLA.

IT'S A DANGEROUS WORLD. YOU AND I *BOTH* GOT REASON TO KNOW THAT. BUT IT DON'T GET BETTER BY *HIDIN'* FROM IT.

IT GETS BETTER WHEN PEOPLE *STAND UP* AN' DO WHAT *NEEDS* DOING. STAND UP TO MAKE IT A *BETTER PLACE.*

LIKE THESE BOYS *RIGHT HERE* DID TODAY.

I CHOPPED COTTON *BEFORE* THE WAR, AND I PEELED TATERS *DURIN'* THE WAR --

-- AND WE BOTH REMEMBER WHAT THERE WAS FOR A COLORED MAN TO COME BACK TO *AFTER* THE WAR.

BUT THERE'S A *NEW WIND* BLOWING, WILLA. MAYBE NOT FOR *US,* BUT --

IT'S FUNNY. WE'D *HEARD* POPPA SAY ALL THAT *BEFORE* --

-- BUT THIS TIME WE *FELT* IT, TOO. MAYBE THE WORLD REALLY *WAS* CHANGING.

EVEN *HERE.* RIGHT *AROUND* US.

WHATEVER. WE'LL NEVER FORGET THAT DAY.

HONOR GUARD, AND THE *BADGE,* AND POPPA *LAUGHING* AND TELLING HOW HE SAW THE ALL-AMERICAN AND SLUGGER IN PARIS, FRANCE.

WE'LL *NEVER* FORGET THAT DAY, ROYAL AND ME.

WE'LL NEVER FORGET THAT *NIGHT,* EITHER.

CHK-CHK

Navy Pilot Testifies
Was Ordered to Bomb
Unauthorized Targets
in North Vietnam

E.A.G.L.E. PLATOON
BATTLES PRAETOR

BOOK ONE

THICKER THAN WATER

It was in Astro City,
in 1972, that it started.

It was late September, a spectacular
Indian summer. One last burst of
paradise before Fall set her teeth
into the world.

Only yesterday, children had shouted
and played in the parks, and the smell
of burning autumn leaves wafted in
from the suburbs.

But that was yesterday,
before fires of a different
sort flared up.

That was
yesterday...

NOoooooooo!

JUST *LOOK* AT IT.

WHAT A WORLD, HUH? LIKE THAT *WITCH* USED TO SAY IN THAT MOVIE.

WHAT A *WORLD.*

ALL RIGHT, YOU KNOW THE *DRILL.* WE MOVE THROUGH FAST, ASSESS THE DAMAGE, FIND OUT WHO NEEDS *MEDICAL ATTENTION.*

WE'VE GOT A LOT OF *GROUND* TO COVER, SO LET'S GO.

THIS IS *CRAZY.* COMPLETELY OUT TO LUNCH.

THINGS LIKE THIS JUST AREN'T SUPPOSED TO *HAPPEN.*

I CAN'T --
MY *MOTHER*,
SHE TURNED
INTO --

-- HOW --
HOW COULD
THIS --

MY WHOLE
BUILDING --
BREATHING --

THEY'RE *STUNNED*.
SHELL-SHOCKED.

I HAD WINGS -- *WASN'T*
HALLUCINATING -- WOKE
UP ON A LEDGE ON THE
NORTH FACE OF
*GRANDENETTI
CATHEDRAL* --

SOMEONE KICKED THE STRUTS
OUT FROM UNDER THEIR *SAFE*,
COMFORTABLE WORLD,
AN' THEY CAN'T *HANDLE* IT.

IDIOTS.

DON'T COME
NEAR ME DON'T
COME NEAR ME
DON'T COME
NEAR ME

HIDING IN A
DUMPSTER, THE
POOR WOMAN.

THIS ISN'T
RIGHT.

MA'AM?

POLICE,
MA'AM.
IT'S OKAY
NOW.

23

-- YOU CAN **SURF** ON IT.

-- APPARENTLY **NOT RELATED** TO **RECENT,** SIMILAR EVENTS IN SAN FRANCISCO --

OUR HEROES -- OUR **SUPERHUMAN GUARDIANS.** OUR PROTECTION AGAINST THE CHAOS. **FAT CHANCE.**

THEY'RE ALL PART OF IT -- THEY CAME INTO OUR LIVES AND BROUGHT IT ALL **WITH** THEM.

PEOPLE CAN'T COUNT ON THE **MASKS** TO FIX THINGS UP FOR THEM.

NO --

-- WE'RE GOING TO HAVE TO DO IT **OURSELVES.**

CHAOS...

CHAOS.

HOOOOONK MBEEPMBEEP HONK

AND IT KEEPS GOING, LIKE ALWAYS.

SUPERHEROES *WAILING* ON EACH OTHER --

-- *GIANT SPIDERS* IN DALLAS --

-- TROLLS PILING OUT OF THE SEWERS IN CITY CENTER --

ELECTRONICS - ST
RADIOS - CAMERAS
CAR STEREOS - WATCHES -
TAPE PLAYERS

STEREOS
CAMERAS

-- YOU GOTTA *LAUGH.*

LIKE IT *MATTERS,* RIGHT? LIKE *ANYTHING* MATTERS.

27

DOESN'T STOP EVERYONE FROM GETTING THEIR *UNDERWEAR* IN A KNOT ABOUT IT. LIKE THE *OLD SOLDIER,* WHEN ALL THAT BREAKS --

WHAT?!

I DON'T *BELIEVE* IT -- !

ASTRO CITY ⚛ ROCKET

TUES OCT 10 1972

OLD SOLDIER FIGHTS FOR NORTH VIET NA

HERE'S THIS GUY, *IMMORTAL* OR WHATEVER, NOBODY'S SEEN HIM SINCE HITLER, HE'S ALWAYS BEEN ONE OF *OUR* BOYS --

-- AND THEN THEY TELL US HE MIGHT BE *BACK,* AND BLOCKING OUR TROOPS FROM MOVING INTO CERTAIN VIET CONG VILLAGES.

YOU FIGURE IT SHOULD BE *BAD ENOUGH,* OLD WHITE MEN SENDIN' YOUNG BLACK MEN TO KILL LITTLE YELLOW MEN, BUT --

-- BUT NO, IT'S ONLY WHEN A *COSTUME* IS INVOLVED THEY GO NUTS --

-- *OUTRAGEOUS* INTERFERENCE WITH NATIONAL DEFENSE, IF THIS IS EVEN *TRUE,* AND NOT A COMMUNISTIC TRICK OF SOME --

THAT'S THE *EASY ANSWER,* RIGHT? WHAT IF HE'S STOPPING ANOTHER *MY LAI,* HUH? WE'RE SUPPOSED TO BE AIR SUPPORT ONLY NOW --

THEY SAID LATER IT MIGHT HAVE BEEN *PSYCHIC AFTERSHOCKS* --

-- DELAYED REACTION TO THE *L.S.DEVIANT* THING, THE WAY EVERYBODY GOT HOT AND BOTHERED ABOUT IT.

ME, I THINK WE WERE JUST GETTING *FED UP* -- TIRED OF TAKING WHATEVER THEY FELT LIKE *STICKING* US WITH --

STAY BACK -- *STAY BACK,* PLEASE!

NOTHIN' T'SEE!

BUT PLENTY TO *HEAR* AND *FEEL.*

THE *RUMBLING* THAT SHAKES THE STREETS -- THE SOUND OF *UNCHECKED DESTRUCTION* --

-- AS TWO MONSTERS TEAR APART *CITY HALL* FROM INSIDE --

WHOOM

THOOM

KSSH

MORE PAIN, MORE VIOLENCE. MORE *DANGER.*

AND WE LET THEM DO IT AND SAY THEY'RE *SAVING* US.

PLEASE *STAND BACK* -- FOR YOUR OWN SAFETY!

WE *CANNOT* GUARANTEE YOUR SAFETY IF YOU REMAIN!

NO SUCH THING AS *SAFETY* IN THIS WORLD. ANYONE WHO THINKS SO IS A FOOL. YOU JUST TAKE WHAT YOU *GET* --

AND YOU GET --

OUT-OF-TOWN *IDIOTS*, THAT'S WHAT THEY WERE. DIDN'T THEY *KNOW?* IF YOU WANT TO PULL A JOB OF ANY SIZE AT ALL IN THIS TOWN --

-- YOU HAVE SOMEONE HIT A *GAS STATION*, BREAK SOME *STORE WINDOWS* ACROSS TOWN, GET SOME *DISTRACTIONS* GOING!

MY HEAD'S *RINGING* -- I CAN'T HEAR MUCH --

-- CAN BARELY *MOVE* --

-- BUT I *MAKE* MYSELF.

EVEN THROUGH THE *RINGING*, THOUGH, I HEAR THAT CLOWN FREAK *LAUGHIN'* AT THEM WHILE HE TAKES THEM DOWN --

NOT MY PROBLEM, THOUGH, *IS* IT?

NOT MY *PROBLEM.*

THKASSH   THKASSH

JACK-IN-THE-BOX. ALWAYS CREEPED ME OUT.

HOPPIN' AROUND LIKE SOME CRAZY *WIND-UP TOY,* THAT BIG FAKE SMILE --

NEVER REALLY STAYING STILL -- AND THAT *WHONGY* SOUND HIS SPRING-THINGS MAKE --

THEIR OWN DAMN *FAULT* FOR BEING STUPID. I DON'T OWE THEM ANYTHING.

SO I JUST STAY *HIDDEN* --

STAY HIDDEN IN THE *DARK* -- AWAY FROM IT ALL --

WHLLLAAAAA

-- TILL IT'S *OVER.*

HEY! YOU! STOP!

ROYAL?

SOME --

-- SOMEBODY HELP --

IN OTHER NEWS, THE CONTROVERSIAL *APOLLO ELEVEN* HAVE BEEN REPORTED TO BE *FUGITIVES* AFTER ESCAPING FROM A *FEDERAL RESEARCH FACILITY* IN --

ΞHMPH!Ξ

OH, HERE WE *GO*...

THE *APOLLO ELEVEN.*

THE ONE THING ORDINARY HUMANS HAD TO BE *PROUD* OF. THEY WENT TO THE *MOON*, NO POWERS, JUST BRAINS AND GUTS. AND *NOW* LOOK AT 'EM.

THEY WERE THERE TO SET UP OUR FIRST *MOONBASE*, ONLY THEY FOUND SOMETHING. SOMETHING OLD, SOMETHING *ALIEN*, THAT CHANGED THEM.

NOW THEY SAY THEY'RE MEANT TO BE *AMBASSADORS* FROM THE STARS, FROM SOME DAMN LOFTY *LEAGUE* OF *CIVILIZATIONS* --

-- AND SENATOR FRIEDRICH SAYS THEY'RE *ALIEN SPIES*, PAVING THE WAY FOR AN INVASION, AND THERE'S A LOT *BELIEVE* HIM --

AND ALL I SEE IS, THEY WERE ONCE *HUMAN*, DAMMIT --

THEY WERE ONCE AS HUMAN AS *YOU* OR *ME*, AND NOW --

AND NOW THEY'RE *FREAKS!* AAAH!

GET *USED* TO IT, CHARLES. IT AIN'T LIKE YOU CAN *STOP* IT.

HEY, I *LIKE* THEM. ESPECIALLY THAT COMET-HEAD GUY. HE'S KINDA *SCARY*, THAT BLANK FACE AN' ALL --

-- BUT HE'S GOT ONE CUTE *BEHIND* ON HIM --

LOOK *OUT*, CHARLES. BAD ENOUGH YOU CAN'T GO OUT WITHOUT DUCKIN' *CARS* AN' STUFF --

-- NOW ALIEN SPIES'RE *STEALIN'* YOUR GIRL!

OH, YOU. THEY AIN'T THAT COMMON.

MILLIONS OF FOLKS GO TO WORK AND HOME EVERY DAY IN THIS CITY WITHOUT SO MUCH AS SEEIN' THE *HUMMINGBIRD!*

THEY MAKE THE NEWS 'CAUSE THEY'RE *FLASHY* -- SO DOES *SEAN CONNERY.* BIG WHOOP.

NO, ROYAL'S *RIGHT*, DARNICE. AND THERE'S MORE OF THEM *EVERY DAY*, IT SEEMS.

AND THE ONES THAT DON'T WRECK TOO MUCH --

-- WE TAKE PICTURES OF THEM AND GET THEIR AUTOGRAPHS AND ALL THE TIME THEY'RE JUST MAKING THINGS *WORSE* AND *WORSE.*

ROYAL'S RIGHT?! I DON'T *BELIEVE* IT. HERE YOU TWO -- BEST FRIENDS FOR *YEARS* -- AND I *NEVER* HEARD YOU AGREE ON NOTHING BEFORE.

NOT *ONCE.*

TIME WE SHOULD BE *GETTING* BACK...

AW, NOT *YET.* THE NIGHT'S YOUNG, AND I WANT ANOTHER *ROUND.*

I'M OUT OF *CASH.*

AND I'VE GOT TO HIT THE BOOKS FOR MY *NIGHT SCHOOL* CLASS...

AFTER I HIT THE *JOHN.* BACK IN A MINUTE.

MEN

HEY, *YOU* GOT MONEY, DON'T YOU, ROYAL?

YOU KNOW HOW TO HAVE MORE FUN THAN READING SOME *STUPID BOOK...*

I ... DON'T *KNOW,* DARNICE.

C'MON. ONE *DRINK.*

YOU AFRAID CHARLES WILL *BEAT YOU UP...?*

UH, I GOTTA GO MYSELF...

ROYAL!

ROYAL -- I'M *OVER HERE!*

MEN

YOUR GIRL'S *DRUNK*, CHARLES.

AW, SHE'S OKAY. SHE'S JUST *RELAXING*.

SHE WORKS *HARD*. YOU SHOULD TRY IT SOMETIME.

HAR-DE-*HAR-HAR*.

LOOK, ROYAL.

YOU'VE NEVER DONE MORE THAN *SMALL-TIME* STUFF, AN' OKAY, YOU *KNOW* HOW I FEEL ABOUT THAT --

YEAH, AND YOU KNOW HOW *I* FEEL ABOUT HOW *YOU* FEEL.

YEAH, *YEAH*. IT'S JUST -- THIS *NEW* STUFF YOU'RE GETTING INTO --

IF THIS IS ANOTHER OF YOUR --

NO *JUDGMENTS*. JUST SOMETHING YOU SHOULD KNOW.

THERE'S THIS GUY -- THIS *NEW* GUY --

I JUST SAW THE FIRST REPORTS. HE'S A *COSTUME.* THEY CALL HIM THE *BLUE KNIGHT.*

HE'S *KILLING* PEOPLE, ROYAL, EXECUTING THEM. MOB BOSSES, PROTECTION GUYS -- -- EVEN LITTLE GUYS LIKE *YOU,* ROYAL --

YEAH. *RIGHT.*

EXECUTING PEOPLE.

IT'S NO *JOKE,* ROYAL. THE FILE ON HIM -- YOU SHOULD *SEE* HIS HIT LIST ALREADY. YOU SHOULD BE --

HE'S A *FAKE.* THE POLICE CAN'T CATCH CROOKS, SO THEY MADE UP SOME *BOOGEYMAN.* THE COSTUMES DON'T KILL, CHARLES.

I'M TRYIN' TO *LOOK OUT* FOR YOU. YOU'RE MY *BROTHER* --

YEAH, LIKE YOU MAKE A POINT OF *TELLING* PEOPLE THAT?

OH, AND YOU *DO?*

THEY *DON'T KILL,* CHARLES!

THERE'S NO MONEY FROM THE *ARMORED CAR JOB*, SO I HAVE TO SCRAMBLE A WHILE. I FIND A FEW JOBS -- SOME LEGIT, SOME NOT.

THEY'RE *STILL* GASSIN' ON ABOUT THE OLD SOLDIER --

-- GETTING INTO IT *REALLY GOOD*, TOO.

CHARLES SAID IT'LL *DIE DOWN*, AND MAYBE IT WOULD'VE, IF NOTHING *ELSE* HAPPENED --

AND THEN SOME *SPACE-THING* CALLED *THE TOURIST* SHOWS UP AND TAKES *MOUNT RUSHMORE* AS A SOUVENIR.

THE FIRST FAMILY MAKES HIM *PUT IT BACK*, BUT THEY STOP THE ARMY FROM *CAPTURING* HIM, LET HIM GO FREE --

AND *STARFIGHTER* BUSTS INTO THE SENATE, STARTS BLOWIN' *POLITICIANS* UP.

WHICH IS KINDA COOL, EVEN IF THEY TURN OUT TO BE *ROBOTS*, DOPPELGANGERS CONTROLLED BY *BOSS DIODE* --

AND ANY OF IT WOULD BE OKAY BY *ITSELF*, BUT ALL TOGETHER, WITH THE OLD SOLDIER THING STILL *HANGING*, IT SAYS ONE THING.

WE'RE NOT IN *CHARGE* ANY MORE. THEY'RE PUSHING US *AROUND*, TELLING US WHAT TO DO.

AND IT DOESN'T MAKE IT BETTER THAT THEY'RE *RIGHT* ALL THE TIME.

SOME PEOPLE ARE OKAY WITH IT, BUT A LOT *AREN'T* -- YOU CAN FEEL THE *BARELY-SUPPRESSED ANGER* IN THE AIR --

THERE IS THIS, THE HEAT, THE *ELECTION*, ALL THAT ABOUT WATERGATE IN THE *POST*, AND THE SICK FEELING THAT THINGS ARE GOING *WRONG* --

IT'S ALL OVER THE *COUNTRY*. YOU CAN ALMOST SMELL IT. COMING OFF PEOPLE LIKE *GAS FUMES*.

ALL IT'D TAKE IS A *MATCH*.

CHARLES! CHARLES, GET IN HERE! YOU WANT TO *SEE* THIS!

MUSIC RECORDS

McANN'S BAR SANDWICHE

Hot Plates

-- REPEAT THE STUNNING BULLETIN --

OH MY --

-- THE *SILVER AGENT*, LONG ONE OF AMERICA'S, AND THE WORLD'S, MOST *REVERED* HEROES --

-- HAS BEEN *ARRESTED*, AND CHARGED WITH THE *MURDER* OF A *FOREIGN HEAD OF STATE*.

AND THAT'S IT. THAT'S THE *MATCH*.

WHAT A *WORLD*, HUH?

ROCKET

5 PILOTS FLEW
IN UNOFFICIAL
AIRFIELD RAIDS

CRIMINAL PROSECUTION

THEY SHOWED THE CLIP *OVER* AND *OVER.*

SIC SEMPER TYRANNIS!

-- NEWS TODAY, INTERNATIONAL FUROR OVER THE BLOODY SHOOTING DEATH OF THE MAHARAJAH OF MAGA-DHOR.

THE CONTROVERSIAL MAHARAJAH, KNOWN AT TIMES AS THE "MAD MAHARAJAH" OR "MAHARAJAH OF MENACE," HAS CLASHED WITH THE SILVER AGENT AND HONOR GUARD *NUMEROUS* TIMES --

-- BUT WAS IN PARIS THIS WEEK PURPORTEDLY TO BROKER *PEACE* TALKS IN THE VIETNAMESE CONFLICT --

-- WHEN HE WAS SHOT *FIVE TIMES* BY A MAN ONLOOKERS AND VIDEO EVIDENCE EXPERTS AGREE WAS THE *SILVER AGENT.*

FRENCH AND AMERICAN SECURITY FORCES *CAPTURED* THE AGENT --

-- THOUGH TWO AMERICANS *DIED* IN THE STRUGGLE, AND ONE FRENCH POLICE OFFICER RECEIVED INJURIES HE IS NOT EXPECTED TO *SURVIVE.*

THE MAHARAJAH WAS CONSIDERED AN *UNPRINCIPLED TYRANT* BY MANY, AND THERE HAS BEEN WIDESPREAD SPECULATION THAT HIS "PEACE TALKS" WERE MERELY A PRETEXT FOR SOME STRATAGEM TO *SEIZE POWER* IN THE REGION --

-- BUT HIS ASSASSINATION HAS SPURRED GREAT INTERNATIONAL OUTRAGE AND ACCUSATIONS OF *AMERICAN MISCONDUCT.*

HIS SUCCESSOR TO THE MAGA-DHORIAN THRONE, THE *STEEL SIRDAR,* HAS VOWED *MASSIVE RETALIATION* UNLESS THE AGENT IS --

EXCUSE ME, I'M BEING HANDED A *BULLETIN* --

OH, MY.

I DON'T WANT TO *TALK* ABOUT IT.

PUT ON A MASK, YOU CAN GET AWAY WITH *ANYTHING.*

DID HE *DO* IT? DON'T ASK ME, I *STILL* CAN'T TELL YOU. BUT I CLIPPED THAT PICTURE OF HIM *BEHIND BARS.* STILL GOT IT.

I SAY *FIVE YEARS.* THEY'DA FOUND A WAY TO *GET HIM OFF* IF HE'D JUST STAYED IN JAIL, BUT WITH THIS ESCAPE AND ALL, THEY *GOTTA* SLAP HIS WRIST.

YOU'RE *CRAZY,* ROYAL. THE EVIDENCE, THE WITNESSES --

YOU THINK THAT *MATTERS?* WAKE UP, CHARLIE BOY! HE WAS *WORKIN'* FOR THEM! THIS IS HOW THEY *DEAL* WITH UPPITY RAGHEADS!

THEY'D'VE GIVEN HIM A *MEDAL,* HE DIDN'T GET CAUGHT --

THAT'S *RIDICULOUS* AND YOU --

HEY, BABY, LET'S NOT MAKE THIS *ANOTHER* FIGHT -- YOU TWO DO TOO *MUCH* OF THAT. LET'S GO OUT. DINNER, DANCING... WE'LL HAVE US A *GOOD TIME.*

NOT TONIGHT, DARNICE, I'M *DEAD TIRED.* THE FIRST FAMILY BUSTED UP *OMNICRON* TODAY -- IT TOOK FOREVER ROUNDING UP HIS *ROBO-GUYS* BEFORE ANYONE GOT HURT.

LET'S JUST STAY IN -- THERE'S STUFF I WANT TO *TALK* TO YOU ABOUT --

MY CUE TO *SPLIT,* GANG.

HAVE FUN. YOU FIND ANY OF THAT *"JUSTICE"* CHARLES TALKS ABOUT, YOU LET ME KNOW.

POOR CHARLES. ALL HE WANTED WAS FOR THE WORLD TO MAKE *SENSE.* ME, I HAD SIMPLER DREAMS. A LITTLE *EASY MONEY,* FOR ONE.

I KNEW A GUY WHO KNEW A GUY WHO KNEW A *GUARD* AT *N.R.GISTICS* IN GAINESVILLE --

-- WHO COULD MAKE SURE A SHIPMENT OF SPECIAL E.A.G.L.E. WEAPONRY WENT *UNGUARDED* --

NOW *THIS* IS THE WAY! NO MUSS, NO FUSS, NO *RISK!*

UNLESS THE *BLUE KNIGHT* GETS YA, MARTY! THEY SAY HE *WALKS THROUGH WALLS* --

-- GRABBED JOHNNY THE EAR AND CARRIED HIM DOWN TO *HELL ITSELF.*

I HEARD THERE WASN'T ENOUGH OF *TURO SANDOVAL'S* BOYS TO IDENTIFY.

HE TAKES THE HEADS FOR HIS *SKULL* COLLECTION.

NAH -- THIS GUY I KNOW *SAW* HIM. HE'S IN ARMOR, HE SAID.

EIGHT FEET TALL WITH *GUNS* GROWIN' OUT OF HIS ARMS -- !

THAT DOESN'T MAKE ANY *SENSE!*

EIGHT FEET TALL -- INTANGIBLE -- *EVERYBODY* KNOWS SOMEBODY WHO KNOWS SOMETHING --

-- BUT NOBODY KNOWS THE *SAME THINGS,* DO THEY?

YEAH, BUT *ONE THING'S* FOR SURE, KID.

THERE'S *SOMETHING* OUT --

SHOOM

SHH! BACK --

OH, MAN --!

HE DIDN'T *SEE* US! I THOUGHT I WAS GONNA HAVE A *HEART ATTACK!* HE'S IN L.A. THESE DAYS -- WHAT'S HE DOING *HERE?!*

YOU IDIOT! HE WORKS FOR THE DAMN *COMPANY!*

MAYBE THEIR MAIN OFFICES ARE IN *L.A.* NOW -- BUT THIS IS *THE ASTRO CITY PLANT!* WHAT, YOU FIGURED HE'D NEVER *SHOW UP* AGAIN?

IDIOTS. THEY JUST THINK THINGS'LL STAY THE SAME BECAUSE SOMEONE *TOLD 'EM* SOMETHING ONCE!

THEY DON'T *CHECK*, DON'T ASK. THEY JUST FIGURE IT'S *ALL FINE*.

WHAT IF IT *HAD* BEEN THE BLUE KNIGHT? THEY SAY HE *KILLS* PEOPLE -- I DON'T BELIEVE IT, BUT THAT'S PEOPLE RIGHT *HERE*, PEOPLE LIKE ME, NOT SOME *FLYING-CARPET GUY* IN CENTRAL ASIA --

AND THEY DON'T EVEN *CHECK OUT* THE JOB?

IT WAS MY SECOND CLOSE SHAVE IN THE LAST *WEEK*, SO MAYBE I WAS JUST NERVOUS.

BUT I GET *TIRED* OF IDIOTS.

HEY! *WILLIAMS!*

WALK BACK TO THE *SUBWAY* WITH ME. WE CAN CATCH A BEER BEFORE WE ALL *MEET UP* AGAIN, SPLIT THE TAKE.

SURE.

LOOK, THIS WAS *FREELANCE* FOR ME, BUT I MOSTLY WORK FOR THE SCARPELLIS. MOVIN' PRODUCT, WATCHIN' FOR *TROUBLE.*

THEY'RE LOOKIN' FOR SOME NEW *PEOPLE.* YOU STAYED COOL BACK THERE, THOUGHT THINGS THROUGH.

YOU'VE GOT A GOOD *ATTITUDE,* AND THREE TIMES THE *BRAIN CELLS* OF THOSE OTHER GUYS.

YOU *INTERESTED?*

REALLY?

STEADY WORK, ROOM TO *MOVE UP.* AND I FIGURE YOU FOR A *MOVER.* WHADDYA *SAY?*

WHO DO I HAVE TO *KILL?*

I FIGURED, WHAT DO YOU *KNOW?* THE WORLD THROWS YOU A *BONE* SOMETIMES.

A CRAZY WORLD, AN' YOU TAKE WHAT *COMES.* FIGURED I'D CATCH A *WAVE* FOR A WHILE, SEE WHAT IT BROUGHT. DIFFERENT *KIND* OF IDIOTS, MAYBE.

IDIOTS.

A *HOSTAGE SITUATION*, AND A MASKED MORON *INTRUDES* ON IT, AND WHAT DOES MY PARTNER DO?

NOT TO *WORRY*, AMIGOS -- I'LL HAVE 'EM OUT OF THERE IN *TWO SHAKES*, HEY?

THEY LEFT THE TOP FLOOR *UNGUARDED*. I'LL COME AT 'EM FROM *ABOVE* -- YOU JUST BE READY WHEN THEY'RE *COMIN' OUT*, CLEAR?

GERARD St.
ᴋɪɴ Ave.

GOT IT, S.A!

IT'S LIKE THE GUY'S ANOTHER *COP* TO HIM. A *LIEUTENANT* OR SOMETHING.

~Hnh~

WHAT?

THIS WHAT THEY TAUGHT YOU AT THE ACADEMY, SIMMONS? JUST LET *ANYONE* WALK INTO A CRIME SCENE?

HEY, THAT'S THE *STREET ANGEL*. HE'S --

YEAH, MAYBE HE *CAN* HANDLE IT. LET HIM *TRY*, MAKE HIM A *BIG SHOT* IF HE PULLS IT OFF.

TELL THE WORLD WE CAN'T HANDLE IT *OURSELVES*, WE POOR DUMB COPS NEED HELP FROM THE *MASKS*.

BUILD HIM UP LIKE THE *AGENT*. AND THEN WHO DOES *HE* KILL, HM?

THIS WAS BACK WHEN THE STREET ANGEL WAS *NEW*, WHEN HE WAS CHEERFUL, JOKEY. BEFORE *BLACK VELVET*.

I DIDN'T KNOW HOW *PROPHETIC* I WAS BEING. BUT THERE WAS A *LOT* WE DIDN'T KNOW, BACK THEN.

54

-- PROTESTERS ON *BOTH SIDES* OF THE VOLATILE *SILVER AGENT* ISSUE -- SOME URGING THE GOVERNMENT TO LET HIM *CLEAR HIS NAME* --

NOT GUILTY

String Him Up

-- SOME DEMANDING *SWIFT JUSTICE,* MORE FOR THE *AMERICANS* KILLED THAN FOR THE *MAHARAJAH.*

HONOR GUARD HAS FORMALLY REQUESTED THAT THE AGENT'S *ARREST WARRANT* BE SUSPENDED WHILE THEY SEEK ANSWERS --

-- BUT SO FAR, THE GOVERNMENT HAS REFUSED TO *CONSIDER IT.*

ATTAWAY, GREEDY OLD WHITE GUYS! DO SOMETHING *SMART* FOR A CHANGE! SOCK THAT CHAINMAIL CHUMP INTO *JAIL!*

OH, ROYAL, YOU DON'T *MEAN* THAT -- !

LIKE *HELL* I DON'T. HEY, TY -- YOU'RE *SLOWIN' DOWN!* ANOTHER ROUND FOR THE *HOUSE!* ON ME, ON *ME!*

COME INTO *MONEY,* HUH? GETTING IN WITH THE *SCARPELLIS,* I HEAR. ROYAL, HOW FAST YOU WANT TO GET YOURSELF *KILLED,* HUH? IS THAT WHAT YOU'RE *TRYING* FOR?

WELL, I COULD *WORK* HARD, GET ME A NICE *APARTMENT,* GO TO CHURCH AND PAY MY *TAXES* ON TIME.

YOU FIGURE *THAT'D* KEEP ME SAFE?

LOOK, ROYAL, LET'S NOT *DO* THIS. I'VE GOT SOME NEWS -- NEWS ACTUALLY WORTH *CELEBRATING*.

ME AND DARNICE, WE'RE GOING TO GET *MARRIED* --

HUH?

DON'T BE AN *IDIOT*, CHARLES.

WHAT -- ?

SHE'S *PLAYING* YOU, MAN. YOU WANT THE HOUSE AND THE PICKET FENCE AND TO KID YOURSELF THE WORLD'S ALL *HAPPY* AND *NICE* --

-- SO YOU WON'T LET YOURSELF *SEE* IT, SEE SHE'S JUST A *GOLD-DIGGER*.

SHE WANTS YOUR *MONEY*, CHARLES, NOT YOU. ONCE IT'S GONE, SHE'S ON TO THE *NEXT* GUY.

YOU DON'T KNOW WHAT YOU'RE *TALKING* ABOUT. YOU JUST CAN'T SEE ANYTHING BUT *BAD* IN PEOPLE --

-- SO YOU THINK EVERYONE'S AS SLIMY AND UNDEPENDABLE AS YOU!

LOTTA *GOOD* OUT THERE I'M MISSING, HUH? *NOTICED* ANY LATELY?

SHH, SHH!

DON'T CRY, DON'T CRY -- HE'LL *HEAR* YOU --

AH, I DON'T KNOW WHY I BOTHER EVEN *TALKING* TO YOU!

WASN'T 'CAUSE I *ASKED* YOU TO --

ROYAL WAS RIGHT ABOUT *ONE THING*, AT LEAST --

-- THERE WASN'T A LOT TO *CHEER* ABOUT IN THE WORLD.

THE *FIRST FAMILY* STOPPED AN INVASION FROM *MONSTRO CITY* --

SOME GUY NAMED *TYRANOS REX.* SON OF MADAME MAJESTRIX, LEADING AN ARMY OF *MONSTERS.*

ONE *MORE* ENEMY TO GUARD AGAINST.

AND EVEN WITH THE WHOLE *SILVER AGENT* FUSS, THERE WERE *NEW* GUYS SHOWING UP. LIKE *HELLHOUND.* THERE'S A CHEERY NAME.

THEY SAID HE WAS A *VIETNAM VET* CAUGHT UP IN SOME SORT OF BLACK-MAGIC THING OVER THERE, *TRANSFORMED.*

AND IF *HE* WASN'T ENOUGH, THE EUROPEAN MAGICIAN, *SIMON MAGUS,* MOVED TO SHADOW HILL.

HE SAID A TIME OF *STRIFE* WAS COMING, AND WE'D BE AT THE *CENTER* OF IT. *THAT* HAD EVERYONE EAGER FOR THE FUTURE, I'LL TELL YOU.

AND THE *APOLLO ELEVEN* WERE INVOLVED IN SOME SORT OF *"CELESTIAL CONVERGENCE."*

SOMETHING TO DO WITH AN *"OMNI-BRAIN."* I STILL DON'T KNOW IF THEY SAVED THE *WORLD,* OR JUST FAILED TO TAKE US ALL *OVER.*

BRIGHT SHINY DAYS, TO LOOK BACK ON WITH *JOY.*

WHEN THE SILVER AGENT FINALLY WENT DOWN, IT WAS *STARFIGHTER* WHO DID IT.

WELL, SORT OF.

THE *STERLING FOUNDATION* -- A GROUP THAT SAID THEY WERE A THINK-TANK OF *BUSINESS LEADERS* AND *SCIENTISTS* --

THEY CAPTURED STARFIGHTER AND CONTROLLED HIM WITH WHAT THEY CALLED A *"MENTAL REGULATOR"* -- AND SENT HIM AFTER THE AGENT.

THEY FOUGHT IN A RUN-DOWN PARK JUST NORTH OF THE SWEATSHOP, AND THE AGENT ACTUALLY *BEAT* STARFIGHTER --

-- BUT BY THE TIME HE DID, THEY WERE SURROUNDED BY *COPS* AND *E.A.G.L.E.* TROOPERS.

THE AGENT *SURRENDERED.*

59

I **HAVEN'T** KILLED **ANYONE.** AND I WON'T START A BATTLE THAT MIGHT LEAD TO THESE FINE MEN GETTING **INJURED** OR **WORSE.**

NOT JUST TO SAVE **MYSELF.**

I WILL LEAVE THE FIGHT TO CLEAR MY NAME TO MY **FRIENDS** AND ALLIES. I HAVE EVERY **CONFIDENCE** THEY'LL PREVAIL.

I ONLY HOPE IT WILL BE IN **TIME.**

I WAS A PART OF IT, BUT ONLY ON THE **FRINGES.**

YOU HARDLY EVER **SEE** ME, IN ALL THE FOOTAGE OF THAT SCENE, ALL THE TIMES THEY'VE SHOWED IT **SINCE** --

MAN, YOU WERE RIGHT **THERE,** ARMED AN' EVERYTHING. DAMN **SHAME.**

ROYAL, I DON'T **GET** YOU.

I KNOW CHARLES DOESN'T **LIKE** HIM -- HE DOESN'T THINK ANY OF THE COSTUMED GUYS SHOULD **EXIST.**

BUT WHY YOU? THE AGENT'S A HERO. WHAT'VE **YOU** GOT AGAINST HIM? WHAT'D HE EVER DO TO **YOU?**

LONG STORY.

GOTTA GO.

SUPPORTERS OF THE SILVER AGENT WILL BE HOLDING **CANDLELIGHT** VIGILS ACROSS THE NATION TONIGHT, WHILE OTHERS REJOICE THAT --

WHEN THE TRIAL OF THE SILVER AGENT STARTED, IT WAS LIKE THE CITY HELD ITS *BREATH*. MAYBE THE *WHOLE WORLD*.

-- PROSECUTION MADE ITS *OPENING STATEMENT* IN THE MURDER TRIAL OF *ALAN JAY CRAIG*, NOW REVEALED TO BE THE MAN BEHIND THE MASK OF THE *SILVER AGENT* --

NOBODY TALKED ABOUT *ANYTHING ELSE*. IT WAS LIKE NOBODY *CARED* ABOUT ANYTHING ELSE.

THE PROTESTERS KEPT *AT* IT -- THERE WERE EVEN *FIGHTS* BETWEEN THEM --

Make Him Pay

One law for ALL

Criminals must Pay

Not Above the LAW

MIND CONTROL

He Didn't Do It

BUT FOR THE *REST* OF US, LIFE WAS ON HOLD --

Let him Clear His Name

NO *WAY* HE DOES JAIL TIME. HIS HONOR GUARD BUDDIES, THEY'LL COME UP WITH *SOMETHING*, YOU'LL SEE.

I DUNNO, TY. HE *EMBARRASSED* THE GOVERNMENT -- FIRST HE KILLS A GUY AT SOME PEACE TALKS, THEN WE CAN'T *HOLD* HIM --

I SHOULD'VE *KNOWN* ... SHOULD'VE FOUND OUT *MORE*...

WHAT DO *YOU* THINK, ROYAL?

EVEN IF THEY COME UP WITH EVIDENCE SAYS HE WAS UNDER SOMEONE'S *CONTROL*, WOULD THEY LET HIM --

-- ROYAL?

OKAY, EVERYONE WAS HOLDING THEIR BREATH BUT *ROYAL*. I JUST FIGURED HE WAS INTO HIS OWN *MESSES*, LIKE USUAL --

-- AND WENT BACK TO THE *SHOW.*

-- DENOUNCED THE UNITED STATES AT *THE U.N.* TODAY, CALLING THE PROCEEDINGS A *"SHAM TRIAL"* OF A *"GOVERNMENT ASSASSIN"* --

THE RUSSIANS WANTED US TO TURN THE AGENT OVER TO A *WORLD COURT.* THE FRENCH, THE BRITISH, A LOT OF THE OTHERS *AGREED.*

NIXON SAID *NO,* THOUGH. WE'D HANDLE IT OURSELVES.

A LOT OF PEOPLE *LIKED* THAT. THEY WANTED US TO STAND UP, TO SHOW SOME *STRENGTH.*

THE FIRST FAMILY PROTECTING THAT *REX* GUY DIDN'T HELP -- THEY SAID HE'D CHANGED HIS *WAYS,* COULDN'T BE BLAMED FOR THE ATTACK.

LIKE HE COULD JUST SAY *"I'M SORRY,"* AND THAT MADE IT *OKAY.*

ANOTHER *TIME,* MAYBE IT'D HAVE GONE DOWN BETTER. NOT THEN, THOUGH.

-- GLAD YOU *ASKED* ME THAT, CHERYL. WE AT THE STERLING FOUNDATION --

WE THINK *NO ONE* SHOULD BE ABOVE THE LAW.

WEARING A MASK SHOULDN'T LET YOU DECIDE WHO *LIVES* OR *DIES,* THAT MONSTERS SHOULD ROAM FREE BECAUSE YOU *LIKE* THEM --

EVEN THE *OTHER* NEWS WAS BAD.

THAT GIANT STONE CREATURE CAME TO LIFE IN VIETNAM, KILLING *DOZENS* OF AMERICAN TROOPS BEFORE THE N-FORCER STOPPED IT.

THE NEWS ABOUT WATERGATE, THE *DROUGHTS* --

WE WANTED A *VICTORY.* SOMETHING, SOMEWHERE, TO FEEL *GOOD* ABOUT.

≹huhh≹

≹huhh≹

I THINK WE LOST -- *AHH!*

JERRY! JERRY, YOU GOTTA GET ME *OUT* OF HERE!

I DON'T GOT MUCH *MONEY* LEFT, BUT --

AAAH!

HE WAS *AFTER* ME. AFTER ANYONE WITH EVEN A *TOUCH* OF THE SCARPELLI MOB.

HE WAS *RELENTLESS,* HE NEVER STOPPED. NOBODY COULD HIDE, NOBODY COULD *ESCAPE* HIM.

CHARLES!

YOU GOTTA -- YOU'LL PROTECT ME, HE WON'T HURT A *COP* -- NOBODY'S *WATCHING* THIS PLACE, RIGHT?

ROYAL, WHAT --

WHAT ON *EARTH* ARE YOU --

CAN'T *SEE* ANYONE, BUT THAT DOESN'T MEAN --

WAIT, WHAT'S THAT ON YOUR *NECK?*

HUH?

IT'S *GLOWING.* IT'S LIKE A -- -- LIKE A *GUNSIGHT* --

OH GOD, OH GOD, IT WON'T COME *OFF* -- IS IT *COMING OFF?*

NO, IT --

GOTTA *HIDE* IT, BLOCK IT, SO HE *CAN'T* --

TINFOIL! MAYBE IT'S RADIO WAVES, MAYBE HE'S A DAMN *ALIEN* --

TINFOIL?

THE TINFOIL ACTUALLY *WORKED.* CHARLES SAID IT MADE THE SYMBOL FADE. BUT TAKE IT OFF, AND IT *CAME BACK* --

HE *MARKED* ME SOMEHOW. MARKED US ALL --

ROYAL. *TELL* ME.

WHAT'S GOING ON?

I TOLD HIM. *ALL* OF IT.

OH, ROYAL...

I DIDN'T *KNOW,* ALL RIGHT? *I DIDN'T KNOW!*

WHAT DO I *DO,* HUH? YOU'RE THE *SMART* ONE, YOU WENT TO COP SCHOOL. WHAT DO I *DO?*

WELL, HE'S NEVER BEEN SIGHTED OUTSIDE THE *CITY* --

HE ALMOST GOT ME AT THE *BUS DEPOT.* HE GOT *LEMMIE* AT THE TRAIN STATION.

I DON'T WANT TO EVEN *THINK* ABOUT BOOSTING A CAR -- HELL, I DON'T WANT TO THINK ABOUT *JAYWALKING!*

CHARLES. I DON'T *KILL* PEOPLE. DON'T EVEN *BEAT* PEOPLE *UP.* I NICK *PURSES.* MOVE BOXES THAT FELL OFF OF TRUCKS. HELP *STEAL* THINGS. I DON'T DO ANYTHING WORTH DYING FOR!

NOT *DYING!*

WELL, I HATE TO SAY IT, BUT MAYBE YOU SHOULD HAVE *THOUGHT* OF THAT BEFORE --

DON'T *SAY* THAT! *DON'T YOU SAY THAT!!*

THIS IS *JUSTICE?* THAT'S WHAT YOU'RE SAYING? I *DESERVE* TO GET SHOT AND LEFT IN AN ALLEY?!

GO ON, TELL ME YOU THINK THERE'S *ANY SUCH THING* AS --

HEY! DON'T YOU TALK TO *ME* ABOUT --

THIS JUST IN...

A *VERDICT* HAS BEEN REACHED IN THE MURDER TRIAL OF ALAN JAY CRAIG, THE SILVER AGENT.

THE JURY CAME BACK AFTER DELIBERATING FOR SIX DAYS, AND RENDERED A VERDICT --

-- OF *GUILTY.*

SHH, ROYAL, *SHH!*

DON'T *CRY* --

CASUALTIES OF WAR

"YOU SHOULDA *SEEN* IT. HE DIDN'T EVEN *SLOW DOWN.*

"LIKE IT WAS JUST SOMETHING THAT *HADDA* BE DONE, AN' HE WAS GONNA *DO* IT, AN' THAT'S ALL THERE WAS *TO* IT.

"IT WAS A *MOBSTER'S* KID, TOO. BY RESCUING IT, HE ENDED A GANG WAR, AND GOT EVIDENCE THAT PUT A BUNCH OF REAL *HARD CASES* AWAY.

"I WOULDA *SWORN* HE WAS A GOOD GUY THROUGH AND THROUGH.

"WHO *KNEW?*"

"I *STILL* CAN'T REALLY BELIEVE IT. HE PULLED MY *MA* OUT OF A CAR WRECK ONCE.

"SHE'D HAD A *SNOOTFUL,* AN' IT WAS ALL HER FAULT, BUT SHE SAID HE NEVER STOPPED TALKIN' TO HER. TELLIN' HER TO *RELAX,* IT'D BE OKAY.

"BUT I GUESS --"

MAYBE GUYS LIKE THAT, THEY START TO FEEL LIKE *GODS* OR SOMETHING, THINK THEY KNOW *BETTER* THAN ANYONE ELSE.

I COULD DO THOSE THINGS, I'LL TELL YOU, *I* SURE WOULD...

THERE WAS A LOT OF TALK ABOUT THE *SILVER AGENT,* THAT WINTER. A LOT OF OLD STORIES TOLD.

WHAT DO YOU *FIGURE?* TEN YEARS? TWENTY?

'SGONNA BE *LIFE,* I TELL YOU. GOTTA KEEP THE GOOKS HAPPY. *AND* THE COMMIES.

A LOT OF PEOPLE DIDN'T WANT TO THINK HE'D DONE IT. BUT THE *EVIDENCE* THAT HAD COME OUT AT HIS TRIAL --

THE WAY HE'D SET UP A *PHONY MEETING* BETWEEN THE MAHARAJAH AND LE DUC THO -- THE WAY HE'D USED *E.A.G.L.E. PRIORITY* TO SLIP IN --

THE WAY HE'D LAIN IN *WAIT,* AND THEN --

ASTRO CITY ROCKET

TUES FEB 27 1973

15¢ DAILY

GUILTY

HINGTON, DC] After deliberating days, the jury returned a guilty on all counts in the murder trial Jay Craig, better known as the itated murder of the Maharajah or in Paris, only weeks ago. have asked for a sentence of trocution, and a sen...

HE WAS GUILTY. MOST PEOPLE *ACCEPTED* THAT.

IT WAS JUST DOWN TO *SENTENCING.*

HE'D MESSED UP THE PARIS *PEACE TALKS* SOMETHING FIERCE. HERE IT WAS LATE FEBRUARY AND THEY WEREN'T *DONE.*

WORD WAS, *THO* WOULDN'T SIGN UNLESS THE AGENT GOT THE DEATH PENALTY, AND *THIEU* WOULDN'T SIGN UNLESS THO DID.

AND WE JUST WANTED *OUT.* OUT OF VIETNAM AND DON'T LOOK *BACK.*

THE PROTESTERS WE SAW ON THE *NEWS* EVERY NIGHT --

THE *ANTIWAR* GUYS WERE THERE. THE GUYS WHO WANTED THE MASKS *SLAPPED DOWN* WERE THERE.

NO ONE ABOVE THE LAW

GUILTY

END THE WAR

Bring Our Boys Home

THE GUYS WHO *BELIEVED* IN THE AGENT WHEN HE SAID HE WAS INNOCENT -- THEY'D *GIVEN UP.*

IT WAS FINE WITH *ME.* GO AHEAD AND *KILL* HIM, IF THAT'S WHAT IT TOOK.

BUT THEN, THEY'D NEVER HAVE LET ME *SERVE* ON THAT JURY.

AND I HAD *OTHER* THINGS TO THINK ABOUT, ANYWAY.

DELI

ROYAL?

75

MAN, IT *TOOK* YOU LONG ENOUGH!

THREE SUGARS, RIGHT? AND NO *MUSTARD* ON THE BURGERS, YOU *KNOW* I HATE MUSTARD.

I THOUGHT I'D *STARVE* TO DEATH WAITING!

WE COULDN'T GET THAT *THING* OFF ROYAL'S NECK, THAT GUNSIGHT THAT MARKED HIM FOR THE *BLUE KNIGHT.*

TINFOIL MADE IT *FADE,* AND KEEPING HIM *UNDERGROUND* BLOCKED IT TOO --

-- BUT WHENEVER HE *SURFACED,* THERE IT WAS AGAIN, BRIGHT AS BRASS. SO HE STAYED HIDDEN.

AND GUESS WHO *WAITED* ON HIM?

OH, *THANK YOU,* CHARLES, YOU'RE A *GOOD* BROTHER, I DON'T KNOW *WHAT* I'D DO WITHOUT YOU.

AW, YOU ONLY DO IT 'CAUSE YOU'D MISS MY *PEARLY SMILE.*

GOT THE *PAPER?* RADIO SIGNAL DOWN HERE IS *CRAPTASTIC.*

SO. THEY MIGHT *FRY* THE BASTARD, HUH? WE COULDN'T BE THAT *LUCKY.*

TUES. FEB 27 1973 ASTRO CITY ★ ROCKET
GUILTY
VERDICT SHOCKS NATION

I DON'T KNOW. IT'S *DIFFERENT* OUT THERE. EVEN *CRAZY JENNY'S* STOPPED SAYING HE'S INNOCENT, AND SHE *WORSHIPS* THEM.

NAH. HONOR GUARD'LL FIND EVIDENCE THAT *CLEARS* HIM, YOU'LL SEE. OR THEY'LL *PLANT* IT. THEY ALL STICK TOGETHER, YOU *KNOW* THAT.

I DIDN'T ARGUE. I'D SAID PRETTY MUCH THE SAME THING THE OTHER DAY, AT THE PRECINCT.

WELL, I SHOULD --

YOU NEVER *TOLD* HER.

WHAT?

DARNICE ASKED ME HOW COME I DON'T LIKE THE *SILVER AGENT*. YOU HAVEN'T TOLD HER ABOUT IT.

ROYAL, DON'T *START* WITH --

NOT *STARTIN'* NOTHING, I'M JUST SAYING...

YOU THINK I DON'T *KNOW* WHAT YOU'RE SAYING?

CHARLES --

YOU THINK I'M SOME DAMN FOOL?

YOU THINK DARNICE IS *NO GOOD,* AND I'M A *FOOL* FOR MARRYING HER WHEN SHE DOESN'T MEET YOUR *OH-SO-LOFTY* STANDARDS, WHEN *YOU'LL* JUMP ANYTHING IN *NYLONS!*

YOU -- YOU --

YOU JUST DON'T WANT ME *GETTING OUT!* BUILDING SOMETHING, BUILDING A *LIFE!* YOU DON'T WANT TO LOSE YOUR *PROTECTION!*

YOU'RE SCARED I WON'T BE THERE TO BRING YOU *BURGERS,* CLEAN UP YOUR MESSES -- HIDE YOU FROM *PSYCHO KILLERS!*

YEAH?

WHO *ASKED* YOU TO, HUH? I DO *FINE!* I GET BY, I HAVE A *GOOD TIME,* AND I'M NOT CHASING STUPID *DREAMS* ALL THE TIME!

YEAH, *LOOK* AT YOU. DOING SWELL IN A DRAFTY BASEMENT WITH A *REYNOLDS WRAP* SCARF.

I DON'T *NEED* YOU! ALL MY LIFE, YOU'VE BEEN PUSHING, *PUSHING,* WITH THE LECTURES AND THE *RULES!*

YOU THINK I CAN'T MAKE IT WITHOUT *MISTER BIG SHOT COP BROTHER? TRY* ME!

GUILTY

FINE. YOU *WANT* TO GET SHOT BY THE BLUE KNIGHT? WHAT THE HELL, YOU BROUGHT IT ON YOURSELF. HE ONLY KILLS *SCUMBAGS* ANYWAY.

I'M *DONE* WITH YOU, ROYAL. YOU'RE ON YOUR *OWN.*

HAVE A NICE *LIFE.*

ME AND CHARLES, WE BLEW UP *FAST.*

IT WASN'T *DARNICE,* NOT MOSTLY. IT'D BEEN COMING FOR YEARS. YEARS OF HIM TRYING TO *PUSH ME AROUND,* AND ME *DISAPPOINTING* HIM.

BESIDES, DARNICE *WAS* NO DAMN GOOD, AND HE *WAS* A FOOL FOR MARRYING HER. SHE DIDN'T WANT TO BUILD *ANYTHING.* NOT HER.

HE JUST WANTED TO PROTECT ME. I *KNEW* THAT. BUT WHAT HE DIDN'T KNOW WAS, HE *COULDN'T* DO IT. NO ONE CAN PROTECT *ANYONE.*

BLACK CAESAR

HE CAME UP FOR *SUPPLIES* EVERY NOW AND THEN.

BUT IF WE SAW EACH OTHER, HE'D CROSS THE STREET. *FINE WITH ME.* LET HIM STAY OUT OF MY PATH.

JOE DON BAKER

WALKING TALL

Charles Bronson is AGENT Z in EYES OF FIRE

GOD, HE LOOKED *PATHETIC.*

I DIDN'T *NEED* HIM.

ALL I HAD TO DO WAS *WAIT* IT OUT.

WAIT UNTIL THAT THING ON MY NECK *FADED.* UNTIL THE KNIGHT WENT ON TO *SOMETHING ELSE.*

I WAS JUST *SMALL POTATOES,* HE COULDN'T STICK ON ME FOREVER.

I HAD A LITTLE *CASH* STASHED, I COULD WAIT IT OUT.

IT GOT *COLD* DOWN THERE, BUT I HAD FOOD, I HAD BEER. A TV WITH AN *ANTENNA* RUN UP IN THE ALLEY WOULD PASS THE --

PT CHAKK

AAAH!

AAA NAAAAA--

I LOST HIM IN THE *SEWERS* AGAIN. I DON'T KNOW IF IT WAS THE PIPES OR THE TINFOIL.

79

I WENT BACK FOR THE TV AT DAWN. IT STILL *WORKED*, MOSTLY.

AND IT WAS A *SHOW*, ALL RIGHT.

NIXON MADE AN *ADDRESS*, TOLD THE COUNTRY THE AGENT MESS WAS "A *CRUCIAL MOMENT*, A MOMENT FOR DELIBERATION, FOR *JUSTICE*."

HE HAD AIDES PLEADING *GUILTY*, BEING CONVICTED LEFT AND RIGHT OVER WATERGATE. WHO'D BELIEVE A *WORD* HE SAID?

BUT THEY *WANTED* TO.

THEY WANTED *SOMETHING*. JACK-IN-THE-BOX CAUGHT *RICHIE FORGIONE*. DRUG TRAFFICKING. LOOKED LIKE THE FORGIONES WERE *DONE*.

BUT THE WITNESSES *VANISHED*, AND RICHIE WALKED.

HE ALWAYS KNEW HOW TO HAVE A *GOOD TIME*, BUT YOU DIDN'T WANT TO SIT TOO *CLOSE* -- BOY HAD A TEMPER.

THE *U.N.* AND *E.A.G.L.E.* HAD TOLD HONOR GUARD TO STAY OUT OF KHANISTAN --

-- BUT WORD WAS THEY WERE THERE *ANYWAY*, STILL TRYING TO CLEAR THE AGENT. IT LOOKED LIKE IT MIGHT BLOW THE PEACE TALKS *AGAIN*.

ONE *MORE* THING FOR THE PUBLIC TO FEEL GOOD ABOUT.

AND THE *FIRST FAMILY*, UP ON THE HILL --

WHERE ARE THEY?!

KRAK

MIIINE... MMMMMIIIINNNEEEE

IT SEEMS THERE WAS THIS *GOVERNMENT* THING ON AN ISLAND OFF THE COAST OF MAINE, SOME *GEOTHERMAL SCIENCE* PLACE.

THEY'D BUILT THIS *WELL*, DOWN THROUGH THE EARTH'S CRUST, AN ENERGY TAP.

BUT *MADAME MAJESTRIX*, THAT *CRAZY* BROAD WHO RULES THE BERMUDA TRIANGLE, SHE KNEW THEY WERE GOING TO WAKE UP THIS THING -- A *MAGMADRAKE* -- AND SHE WANTED IT.

SHE HAD HER MONSTER TROOPS *TAKE OVER* THE INSTALLATION, AND WHEN THE FIRST FAMILY TRIED TO STOP HER, SHE GOT *THEM*, TOO --

-- AND SET THEM UP AS *SACRIFICES*, A GIFT TO THE MAGMA-THING.

NO!

BUT IT TURNS OUT THAT HER *SON*, THAT TYRANOS REX GUY -- WELL, HE WAS JUST A KID, MAYBE 14 YEARS OLD --

-- AN' HE DIDN'T LISTEN TO HIS MAMA. KIDS *TODAY*, HUH?

KRSSHHH

REX, YOU *DID* IT! YOU *DID* IT!

NICK! NATALIE! HOLD THE MAGMADRAKE *BACK* -- I NEED *THREE MINUTES*!

YOU *GOT* IT, DAD!

JULIE! THE WRECKAGE OF THE *TECHNO-ALTAR* -- QUICKLY!

DRAGONS! HMPPH!

YOU -- YOU *DAAARRREEE....*?

DON'T TAKE IT *PERSONALLY*, LONG, HOT AND SCALY -- SHE JUST LIKES *UNICORNS* BETTER!

GIRLS, YOU KNOW?

ALL RIGHT, CHILDREN -- *BACK!*

AND *YOU!* BACK TO THE *DEPTHS*, MONSTER -- AND *RETURN NO MORE!*

HARRRRR

THIS *GRAVITIC PLUNGER* WON'T JUST FORCE HIM DOWN -- IT'LL REALIGN THE MIXTURE IN THE *LAVA* THAT SERVES HIM AS BLOOD --

-- GIVING HIM THE EQUIVALENT OF THE *"BENDS"* IF HE EVER RESURFACES!

YEAH, YEAH. HEY, KIDS -- YOU *OKAY?*

OH, MY FRIENDS -- I AM SO *SORRY.* CAN YOU FORGIVE ME FOR ALMOST *FAILING* YOU -- ?

FORGIVE YOU? REXIE -- YOU'RE THE *BEST!*

SO THE DAY WAS SAVED AND EVERYTHING WAS *ALL RIGHT,* RIGHT?

WELL, NOT *QUITE.*

FIRST OFF, THE GEOTHERMAL PLACE WAS A *WRITE-OFF,* AND THAT MEANT BILLIONS OF TAX DOLLARS WASTED.

AND OUR BIGGEST BRAINS DIDN'T KNOW ABOUT THE *MAGMADRAKE,* SO WE LOOKED PRETTY STUPID ON *THAT* FRONT, TOO.

BUT WORSE, AFTER THAT *REX* GUY RAN AWAY FROM HOME LAST MONTH, THE FIRST FAMILY SHELTERED HIM UNTIL THE *FEDS* STEPPED IN.

HE'D BEEN DECLARED *PERSONA NON WHATEVER,* TOLD HE COULDN'T COME WITHIN U.S. BORDERS, NOT *ANYWHERE,* NOT FOR *NOTHING.*

SO BY SAVING THE DAY, HE'D *VIOLATED* THE GOVERNMENT'S ORDERS.

THE F.B.I. AND E.A.G.L.E. DEMANDED THAT REX BE TURNED OVER TO U.S. CUSTODY FOR *"APPROPRIATE PROCEEDINGS."*

THE FIRST FAMILY TOLD 'EM TO GO *SPIN.*

-- REPORTEDLY MOVED THE CREATURE TO *OUTPOST F,* THEIR ORBITAL BASE, WHICH THEY CLAIM IS *OUTSIDE* U.S. JURISDICTION.

A FEDERAL JUDGE TODAY ISSUED AN ORDER TO *COMPEL* THE FIRST FAMILY TO --

THE THING IS, WE DON'T LIKE TO FEEL LIKE WE'RE NOT IN *CONTROL.*

IN *OTHER* NEWS, THE SENTENCING HEARING FOR THE SILVER AGENT IS SET FOR NEXT WEEK.

REPRESENTATIVES FROM ALL THE *N.A.T.O.* NATIONS WILL BE THERE TO OBSERVE, AND *DIPLOMATIC* STAKES MAY BE HIGH.

FRANCE AND MAGA-DHOR *BOTH* ISSUED DENUNCIATIONS OF --

WE TELL OURSELVES WE'RE *AMERICA.* STRONG. FREE. *LEADERS.*

BUT IT'S HARD TO *BUY* THAT SOMETIMES. FOR ALL THE TALK ABOUT "PEACE WITH HONOR," WE *LOST* IN VIETNAM.

THE TIDE WAS GOING AGAINST NIXON ON *WATERGATE,* TOO. BUT HE WAS STILL OUR PRESIDENT. WHAT WE WERE *LEARNING,* IT HURT.

IT FELT LIKE THE WORLD WAS LOOKING AT US, ASKING HOW WE COULD LEAD IF WE COULDN'T KEEP ORDER AT *HOME.*

IT WAS A *FAIR* QUESTION.

-- GLAD YOU *ASKED* ME.

WE AT THE STERLING FOUNDATION *RESPECT* AND *ADMIRE* OUR NATION'S HEROES. BUT WE CAN'T LET THEM RUN *ROUGHSHOD* OVER US.

WE MUST BE *STRONG.* AMERICA MUST *STAND UP,* AND TAKE CONTROL OF HER DESTINY. *STAND UP* -- OR GET USED TO *LYING DOWN.*

IT WAS THE FIRST TIME I GOT A *HINT* OF IT. THE FIRST TIME I THOUGHT THE SENSE THAT THE MASKS WERE *US* -- WERE PART *OF* US -- WAS SLIPPING.

AND THEN --

THEN --

Stand Up AMERICA ☆

-- RECENTLY-ARRIVED SORCERER *SIMON MAGUS* SAYS THE THREAT OF THE *BLUE KNIGHT* MAY BE --

MAGUS SAID THE KNIGHT HAD BEEN *POSSESSED* -- SOME ANCIENT VENGEANCE SPIRIT TRYING TO BE *REBORN* --

-- BUT HE AND SOME OTHERS BURNED IT *OUT* OF HIM AND HE WAS PROBABLY DEAD. I COULD PRACTICALLY *HEAR* IT --

WOO-HOOOOO!

I *DID* IT! I *DID* IT! I *OUTLASTED* YOU, YOU SKULL-FACED FREAK, YOU *HEAR* ME? I *OUTLASTED* YOU, YOU STINKIN' --

IN OTHER NEWS, OFFICIALS AT THE *E.A.G.L.E.* OMEGA-SECURITY HOLDING FACILITY IN MURFREESBORO, TENNESSEE REPORT --

-- THAT ALAN CRAIG, THE SILVER AGENT, *VANISHED* FROM HIS CELL FOR SIX MINUTES LAST NIGHT, BEFORE REAPPEARING, IN UNIFORM AND --

WHAT?

WHAT?

AND THEN THERE IT *WAS* AGAIN. AS FRESH AS IF IT HAD HAPPENED YESTERDAY. I'M SURE *ROYAL* WAS THINKING ABOUT IT TOO --

IT WAS *1959.*

A *PYRAMID ASSAULT SQUAD* ON THE ROOFTOPS OF BAKERVILLE.

PYRAMID HAD FOUGHT WITH *HONOR GUARD* EARLIER THAT DAY -- A WAR MACHINE, THEY FOUGHT IT ON *MULBERRY STREET.*

ME AND ROYAL, WE SAW IT *ALL.*

BUT THEY'D EJECTED SOME SORT OF *POWER-CORE* THING FROM THE MACHINE, SO IT WOULDN'T BE CAPTURED, THE PAPERS SAID LATER. THEY CAME BACK TO *GET* IT.

SO DID *HE.*

-- TRAFFIC HELICOPTERS REPORTING A *DARING ROOFTOP BATTLE* GOING ON RIGHT NOW, BETWEEN THE SILVER AGENT AND *UNKNOWN FOES* --

ROGERS RADIO

BROADCAST

WE WERE SO EXCITED.

THE AGENT SEEMS TO BE OUTNUMBERED *TEN* OR *TWELVE* TO ONE, BUT -- *OH!* HE'S GOING THROUGH THEM LIKE A *THRESHER*, PETE --

OH, MAN!

DO IT, SILVER AGENT! RIGHT IN THE *FACE!* POW!

YOU BOYS ARE GOING TO HAVE TO TURN THAT *OFF.* IT'S A SCHOOL NIGHT, AND YOU'VE GOT *HOMEWORK* TO --

NOW, WILLA, *LET* THEM --

-- CAN CONFIRM THAT IT'S *PYRAMID* FORCES, YES!

KRAK

THE APPARENT LEADER IS MAKING A *BREAK* FOR IT, FLEEING OVER HERRIMAN STREET, BUT --

HERRIMAN STREET? BUT THAT'S RIGHT --

KRK--

BOYS, LOOK --

HEY! HEY, YOU CAN'T —

BLASTED *ARMORERS!*

I'VE TOLD THEM *BEFORE* — ONE CRACK IN THESE *IDIOTIC* VISORS AND *VISIBILITY* GOES STRAIGHT TO —

KRAK

WHAT? WILLA! **WILLA!**

KRAK

SHRAMMM

Hnh. *BETTER.* AND THERE —

— MAYBE *THAT'LL* SLOW HIM UP A LITTLE —

WHAT'S — WHO —

ROYAL, *NO!*

HE WENT BY -- HE DIDN'T *SEE* US --

WE SAW *HIM,* THOUGH -- WE BOTH DID --

SAW THAT FACE WE'LL NEITHER OF US EVER, *EVER* FORGET --

AND THEN HE WAS GONE, BUT THERE WAS *ANOTHER* ONE --

SHH, *SHH!*

DON'T CRY -- HE'LL *HEAR* YOU --

AND WHEN HE WAS *GONE* -- WE'D SEEN THE GLINT ON HIS ARMOR --

HE'D FIRED *FIRE-EXTINGUISHING-FOAM* BULLETS ON THE WORST OF THE BLAZE --

AND WE REALIZED WHO IT HAD BEEN AND *HOPED,* BUT --

M-MA?

P-POPPA -- ?

THIS WASN'T WHAT WAS *SUPPOSED* TO HAPPEN.

WE COULDN'T *STOP* IT. ALL WE COULD DO WAS HIDE AND *LISTEN* --

HE WAS THE HERO. WE'D BEEN *CHEERING* HIM. HE WAS SUPPOSED TO HAVE SAVED US -- SAVED ALL OF *US* --

DAD? D-*DAD,* ARE YOU -- ?

CHARLES.

BUT HE JUST *WENT BY.* CHASING THE BAD GUY.

HE DIDN'T EVEN *STOP* --

HE DIDN'T EVEN *LOOK BACK.*

HE'S JUST -- HE'S *LEAVING* --

IT WASN'T VERY LONG BEFORE *FIREMEN* CAME. AND POLICE, AND OTHERS. I DON'T KNOW, MAYBE HE'D *CALLED* THEM.

MAYBE HE'D HAVE *STOPPED* IT IF HE COULD --

MAYBE IF HE'D *SEEN* US, KNOWN WE WERE THERE, BUT --

IT'S NOT WHAT WAS *SUPPOSED* TO HAPPEN.

IT'S NOT WHAT WAS SUPPOSED TO HAPPEN.

THAT WAS WHEN CHARLES *WIGGED OUT.* STARTED TO GET *OBSESSIVE* ABOUT THE MASKS, ABOUT HOW WE DIDN'T *NEED* THEM, *SHOULDN'T* NEED THEM, SHOULD TAKE CARE OF *OURSELVES* --

THAT WAS WHEN ROYAL LOST *FAITH.* STARTED TO BELIEVE THAT NOTHING MADE *SENSE,* NOTHING KEPT YOU *SAFE,* SO WHY FOLLOW THE RULES.

YOUR VERDICT IS *UNANIMOUS?*

THE SENTENCE CAME DOWN THE *NEXT DAY.* IT WAS EARLY AFTERNOON. DEATH BY *ELECTROCUTION,* THEY SAID.

TO BE CARRIED OUT *"WITHOUT ANY UNDUE DELAY."*

THE AGENT, JUST GAVE A LITTLE *NOD,* LIKE HE'D BEEN EXPECTING IT.

HIS LAWYER STARTED TO SAY SOMETHING ABOUT AN *APPEAL,* BUT THE AGENT SHOOK HIS HEAD. NO APPEAL.

IT WAS KINDA *QUIET* IN THE CITY THAT DAY.

BUT OVER TIME, PEOPLE STARTED TO *TALK*. TO *REASSURE* EACH OTHER, MAYBE.

WE'D *WANTED* THEM TO DO SOMETHING. TO TAKE ACTION, TO SHOW WE STILL HAD *CONTROL* OF THINGS. OF OUR *COUNTRY*.

IT BROUGHT THE *VIETNAMESE* BACK TO THE TABLE, THEY SAID. NORTH *AND* SOUTH.

SHOWED THE OTHER HEROES THEY COULDN'T JUST GO DO WHATEVER THEY WANTED AND EXPECT A *WALK* ON IT.

AMERICA STOOD UP. AMERICA WAS *STRONG*.

WE *TOLD* OURSELVES THAT. IT WAS A HARD CHOICE, BUT IT WAS THE *RIGHT* CHOICE.

SOMETIMES, THAT'S WHAT YOU'VE GOT TO *DO*.

...FOR THE PURPOSE OF ANNOUNCING THAT WE TODAY HAVE CONCLUDED AN AGREEMENT TO *END* THE WAR AND BRING PEACE WITH *HONOR* IN VIETNAM AND IN SOUTHEAST ASIA.

THE FOLLOWING STATEMENT IS BEING ISSUED AT THIS *MOMENT* IN WASHINGTON AND HANOI...

IT WAS THE *RIGHT CHOICE*. PEOPLE KEPT SAYIN' IT, LIKE THEY WERE TALKIN' THEMSELVES *INTO* IT. IT WAS THE RIGHT DECISION.

AND AT LEAST THIS WAY, IT'D BE *OVER*, THEY SAID.

IT'D BE *OVER*.

...GOT YOU ON *DESK DUTY*, HUH? YOU MUST *LOVE* THAT.

WELL, UNTIL THIS BUSTED *WING* OF MINE HEALS UP, I'M NO GOOD ON THE STREET. I'M STILL *KICKING* MYSELF FOR BEING STUPID.

THIS THE *PLACE?*

YEAH, JOSH, WE CAN JUST GRAB A *BEER* AND --

Ah, LOOK, I KNOW *ANOTHER* PLACE. LET'S...IT'S NEARBY.

SURE, NO SWEAT.

HEY, THAT *SKINNY* GUY IN THERE...

...DO I *KNOW* HIM FROM SOMEWHERE?

IT WAS THE DAY THE *SILVER AGENT* WAS SENTENCED TO DIE.

FRY HIS BUTT

STAND UP USA

THE NEWS SAID THERE WERE *75,000* DEMONSTRATORS CHEERING IT ON. TODAY, YOU'D BE LUCKY TO FIND *50* WHO'D ADMIT BEING THERE.

ME, I'LL *ADMIT* IT...

-- HAS SELECTED HIS *LAST MEAL.*

SIRLOIN STEAK, BAKED POTATO, GREEN BEANS, A CAESAR SALAD -- AND OH YES, *CHOCOLATE LAYER CAKE* FOR DESSERT.

AND A QUART OF *MILK* TO WASH IT DOWN.

THE AGENT HAS BEEN UNDER *24-HOUR VIDEO SURVEILLANCE* SINCE HIS *INEXPLICABLE DISAPPEARANCE* FROM HIS CELL, WEEKS AGO --

ARTIST'S RENDITION

-- AND SUBSEQUENT *REAPPEARANCE,* SIX MINUTES LATER, IN A TATTERED AND GRIMY VERSION OF HIS 'SUPERHEROIC' COSTUME.

COPIES OF THE VIDEO FOOTAGE HAVE BEEN *DENIED* TO NEWS ORGANIZATIONS, EXCEPT FOR *THIS* --

THERE ARE SOME *ROUGH TIMES* COMING.

BUT DON'T WORRY. IT'S GOING TO BE *OKAY.*

≥HMPH!≤ LIKE WE CARE WHAT HE'S GOT TO SAY...

THERE'S BEEN GREAT *DISAGREEMENT* OVER WHAT MAY HAVE BEEN HIS FINAL PUBLIC STATEMENT. DOES HE REFER TO HIS OWN *FATE,* OR --

...IF I *COULDA* SWUNG IT, I NOT ONLY WOULDA *BEEN* THERE, I'D'VE PULLED THE *SWITCH.*

IN OTHER NEWS, THE **FIRST FAMILY,** THE TEAM OF ADVENTURERS HEADED UP BY AUGUSTUS FURST, **CONFIRMED** EARLIER REPORTS TODAY --

-- THAT THEY ARE **SEVERING TIES** WITH ASTRO CITY AND THE UNITED STATES OVER FEDERAL ORDERS TO SURRENDER **TYRANOS REX,** PRINCE OF THE UNDERSEA **MONSTRO CITY.**

PRINCE **REX** COMES TO US SEEKING **ASYLUM,** AS MANY HAVE COME TO AMERICAN SHORES BEFORE.

HE HAS PROVEN HIS GOOD INTENTIONS TO US **MORE** THAN SATISFACTORILY. HE IS MY **BROTHER'S** AND MY **ALLY,** MY CHILDREN'S **FRIEND.**

WE WILL **NOT** ABANDON HIM IN HIS TIME OF **NEED.**

THE FURSTS HAVE RELOCATED TO THEIR ORBITAL BASE, **OUTPOST F.** THE IMMEDIATE DISPOSITION OF THEIR **MOUNT KIRBY** HOME IS **UNKNOWN.**

SCIENTISTS AND AUTHORITIES ARE **PUZZLED** OVER THE APPEARANCE OF APPROXIMATELY 360 MYSTERIOUS **PYLONS** ACROSS THE CONTINENT.

GENERATING INTENSE FIELDS OF AN **UNKNOWN ENERGY,** THE PYLONS HAVE SO FAR **DEFIED** ALL ATTEMPTS AT ANALYSIS.

AFTER APPARENT ATTEMPTS TO DESTROY TWO OF THE PYLONS BY THE CONTROVERSIAL **APOLLO ELEVEN** AND BY **HONOR GUARD** --

-- THE STRANGE ARTIFACTS HAVE BEEN PLACED **UNDER GUARD** WHILE E.A.G.L.E. SCIENTISTS EXAMINE --

AW, **GET ON WITH IT!** WE DON'T CARE ABOUT NO STUPID **PYLONS!** BIG METAL STICKS, SO **WHAT?** GET BACK TO THE AGENT -- LET'S SEE SOME **ACTION!**

WAS A *TIME*, I'D HAVE MADE THE TRIP WITH MY BROTHER *CHARLES*. OR AT LEAST WATCHED IT ALL ON *TV* WITH HIM.

NOW, THOUGH...

I ONLY GOT *FORTY MINUTES* FOR LUNCH, TY.

CORNED BEEF AND A *COKE*, OKAY?

IT WAS PRACTICALLY A *PARTY*, PEOPLE WERE SO CRANKED UP ABOUT IT.

THE AGENT HADN'T MADE ANY *APPEALS.* HADN'T *ASKED* FOR CLEMENCY. NIXON TURNED HIM DOWN *ANYWAY.*

TODAY, THE WORLD SEES THAT AMERICA IS A NATION OF *LAWS,* A NATION OF *JUSTICE.*

WE WILL NOT *TOLERATE* THOSE WHO TAKE THE LAWS INTO THEIR OWN HANDS...

I THOUGHT IT WAS THE *RIGHT THING* TO DO. BUT THE WAY HE WAS DOING IT -- USING IT TO LOOK *STRONG,* TO DISTRACT US FROM *WATERGATE* --

AND THE WAY THE COUNTRY *ATE IT UP* --

LOOK, LOOK! THEY'RE SENDIN' IN THE *PRIEST!*

DO IT! *DO IT!* GO! *GO! GO!*

THIS WAS STILL A MAN'S *LIFE.*

GO! GO! GO! GO! GO! GO!

WHKMM

WH--?

WHAT IN -- ?

G-GOOD *GOD!*

THAT'S WHEN *SHE* SHOWED UP.

103

AND JUST LIKE THAT, THE WAR WAS *ON.*

IT WAS ALMOST *FUNNY.* ONE SECOND, THEY WERE *CHEERIN' ON* THE DEATH OF *ONE* OF THEIR BIG-TIME HEROES, AND THE NEXT --

SHOW 'ER, HONOR GUARD!

SHE CAN'T *THREATEN AMERICANS!*

GO, *FURSTS!* GO, *APOLLO 11!*

SHOW HER WHO'S *BOSS,* YOU, UH -- YOU *MAGNIFICENT ALIEN FREAKS!*

THEY'D EVEN FORGOTTEN TO BE MAD AT THE FIRST FAMILY FOR *STARTIN'* ALL THIS.

I HAD TO WONDER. IF WE *LOST,* WOULD THEY BE CURSIN' THE FURSTS AGAIN AS WE ALL GOT PITCHED INTO *SPACE?*

PROBABLY. WHAT A *WORLD,* HUH?

WHAT A --
-- HM?

AHHH!

WHAT?

STOP IT
STOP IT!

ALL UNITS,
ALL UNITS --

THE *QUAKES* STARTED WHILE THE FIGHT WAS JUST GETTING UNDERWAY. NOT MUCH, AT FIRST, BUT THEY'D *GROW*, WE KNEW IT.

WE WERE *ALL* CALLED IN. CROWD CONTROL, LIKE IT WAS GOING TO DO ANY *GOOD*.

I DID WHAT I *COULD.* MOSTLY JUST GETTING PEOPLE OUT OF THE *DANGER ZONE.*

NOT THAT IT MADE THEM SAFE FROM THE *QUAKES,* BUT AT LEAST THEY WOULDN'T BE TRAMPLED BY *DINOSAURS.*

I WAS LOOKING FOR ANYONE *TRAPPED,* WHEN --

ROYAL...?

WHAT IN -- ?

I DIDN'T *THINK.* I JUST --

THEY SAID HE WAS *DEAD.* HAH. LIKE I SHOULDA *BELIEVED* THEM -- HOW MANY TIMES THEY SAID THAT ABOUT THE *SILVER BRAIN?*

PROBABLY DEAD, THEY EVEN SAID. *PROBABLY!*

I DON'T KNOW WHAT *DROVE* HIM. THE WORLD WAS DYING, AND HE WAS STILL AFTER *ROYAL* --

AND ALL I COULD FEEL WAS *FLAMES* --

OKAY, OKAY, YOU *GOT* ME.

I DON'T -- DON'T KNOW *WHY,* BUT YOU GOT ME.

JUST -- JUST MAKE IT --

NO!

CHARLES?

AND WE MISSED IT ALL, BUT --

EH?

WHOOOOO...

NOT... NOT ALL THAT GOOD A *GUY,* HUH?

YOU GOT A *COMPLAINT?*

I MEAN NO *DISRESPECT*, MOTHER -- TO YOU, *OR TO OUR* NATION. BUT I WILL NOT BE *ORDERED* BY ANOTHER -- ANY MORE THAN *YOU* WOULD BE.

VERY *WELL*, THEN --

-- LET US... *TALK*.

WE DIDN'T KNOW WHAT HAPPENED *NEXT*. I DON'T THINK *ANYONE* DID, EXCEPT THE PEOPLE WHO WERE THERE.

MADAME MAJESTRIX SHUT DOWN HER *INERTIAL BOLTS* AND RETURNED TO MONSTRO CITY.

REX STARTED SPENDING HIS TIME WITH THE *FURSTS*, AND EVENTUALLY JOINED. THEY CAME *BACK* TO THE CITY, IN TIME. IN THE *MEANTIME*, THOUGH --

≡WHEW!≡

HE -- JUST -- THEY -- WE ALMOST --

IT'S OVER -- IT'S *OVER* --

SOMEONE FIND A *PHONE!*

A *TELEVISION!* WHAT'S ON THE *NEWS -- ?!*

TVs · STEREOS HI-FIs

ELECTR

BUT THE NEWS DIDN'T HAVE ANY *SURPRISES.* IT WAS JUST WHAT WAS *EXPECTED* TO HAPPEN. WHAT WAS *SUPPOSED* TO HAPPEN.

HE HADN'T *REQUESTED* CLEMENCY. HE HADN'T *GOTTEN* IT.

ALAN JAY CRAIG, ALSO KNOWN AS THE *SILVER AGENT,* WAS EXECUTED TODAY AT *4:33 PM,* EASTERN TIME.

TWO MINUTES *BEFORE* HE'D APPEARED IN ASTRO CITY.

HUH.

YOU HEARD A *LOT*, AFTER THAT, ABOUT HOW MAYBE HE SAVED THE *WORLD*, OR JUST THE COUNTRY, BUT HE WAS STILL A *KILLER*, RIGHT?

YOU HEARD A LOT ABOUT HOW THE SENTENCE WAS *JUST*, HOW IT WAS WHAT SHOULD HAVE HAPPENED. BUT IT SOUNDED *HOLLOW*.

THAT WAS BEFORE STARFIGHTER BUSTED UP THE *STERLING FOUNDATION*. THEY'D *VANISHED* -- GONE LIKE THEY'D NEVER *EXISTED*.

AND THEIR OFFICES WERE FULL OF *TECHNOLOGY* NEVER BEFORE SEEN ON THIS PLANET.

THAT WAS BEFORE THE *MAD MAHARAJAH* SHOWED UP AGAIN, LARGE AS LIFE AND MOCKING US ALL.

IT WASN'T UNTIL HE *REALLY* DIED, AND HIS *FILES* WERE RECOVERED, THAT WE FOUND OUT WHAT REALLY *HAPPENED*.

THAT IT *WAS* THE SILVER AGENT, BUT HE'D BEEN MIND-CONTROLLED. AND HE'D KILLED A *BIO-DECOY*.

THAT STARTED UP A WHOLE *'NOTHER* ROUND OF TALK, OF *FINGER-POINTING*. ROYAL *STILL* DOESN'T BELIEVE IT.

BUT RIGHT THEN, ALL WE KNEW WAS HE WAS *DEAD* AND WE DIDN'T KNOW *WHAT* TO THINK.

HUH.

AND NOT JUST ABOUT THE *SILVER AGENT*, EITHER.

I COULD SEE IT IN HIS *EYES*. HE'D SAY, "*I DIDN'T ASK YOU,*" AND I'D SNAP BACK, "*I DIDN'T DO IT FOR YOU,*" AND WE'D BE AT EACH OTHER'S THROATS.

I COULD PRACTICALLY *HEAR* IT. I'D SAY, "*SO, THIS MEAN I'M INVITED TO THE WEDDING?*" AND HE'D GIVE THAT HALF-GRIN AND SAY, "*DOES THAT MEAN YOU'RE COMING?*"

BUT --

YEAH...

END OF BOOK ONE

Astro City, 1976.

It had been a long autumn, full of crisp days and cool, lingering evenings, shading slowly into night.

But as early as September, there was the promise of winter. A deeper chill running through the twilight breezes, rustling the fallen leaves with a dry, hungry rattle.

Now it was December. The snows had come on quickly, but it was the cold people felt most.

There was something in the wind...

THE NEWS WAS FULL OF *HUGE* DEVELOPMENTS.

STARFIGHTER AND *HONOR GUARD* HAD SAVED THE INFRA-DAUPHIN FROM SOME VAST *ALIEN ARMADA,* AND GOT INVITED TO WITNESS THE BIRTH OF THE NEW GENERATION OF *UNIVERSALS* AS PAYBACK.

THEY BROUGHT ALONG *TV REPORTERS* WHO FILMED THE WHOLE THING.

THE *FIRST FAMILY* WAS ON AN INTERDIMENSIONAL TOUR OF THE *RING OF WORLDS,* MEETING ADVENTURERS AND DIGNITARIES FROM OVER A DOZEN REALITIES.

THE FAN MAGAZINES WERE ALL *OVER* THAT, OF COURSE.

STARWOMAN HAD RETURNED TO EARTH BRIEFLY, TO STAVE OFF THE *DARK AURORA.*

IT WAS THE TURNING POINT IN SOME *INTERSTELLAR WAR* OR OTHER.

AND THE *APOLLO ELEVEN* SAVED AUSTRALIA FROM THE GOLDEN HORDE, NOT THAT THEY GOT MUCH *THANKS* FOR IT.

MOST OF US IN THE *CITY,* THOUGH -- WE DIDN'T PAY TOO MUCH *ATTENTION.*

WE HAD *OTHER THINGS* TO DEAL WITH.

A COLD WIND BLOWING

I'D JUST RECENTLY STARTED WORKING *MAJOR CRIMES.* LAST PLACE I WANTED TO BE, BUT THE *MONEY* WAS BETTER.

MY PARTNER *LANNIE* WAS SHOWING ME THE ROPES. SUCH AS THEY *WERE.*

LANNIE! SOMETHING'S STILL MOVING IN --

KSSH

TSSH

UH-OH --

IT WAS THE *JADE DRAGONS.*

I WAS BRINGING MY GUN UP, ABOUT TO TELL 'EM TO *FREEZE,* WHEN --

133

I'D FOUND MY WAY INTO WORKIN' FOR *JOEY "THE PLATYPUS" PLATAPOPOULOUS*, WHO RAN CRIME IN THE SWEATSHOP.

BUT SOME OF THE *OTHER BOSSES* HAD BEEN PUSHIN' INTO HIS TURF, AND HE WAS PUSHIN' *BACK*.

SO WE GET *HALF* THE NUMBERS RECEIPTS TONIGHT, HUH? *HALF.* GUNN'S DAMNED *GUNBIRDS* GOT THE OTHERS?

NO *MORE* O' THIS, I SAY. *HEAR* ME?

DEKE? YOU MAKE THE *CALL?*

SEVERAL CALLS, SIR.

I EXPLAINED OUR CURRENT... *DIFFICULTIES* TO OUR FRIENDS IN CHICAGO, AND THEY ARE AS *CONCERNED* AS WE ARE. THEY *AGREE* THAT SOMETHING MUST BE DONE.

THEY ARE SENDING AID -- IN THE PERSON OF *JITTERJACK*, THE *DIVIDED MAN.*

JITTERJACK? MAN, *THAT* PSYCHO?! WELL, *AWRIGHT* -- *THAT'LL* SHOW 'EM!

JITTERJACK?

THEY WERE BRINGING IN *JITTERJACK?* I WISHED I COULD GO BACK TO *CREDIT CARD FRAUD*, OR BOOSTING CAR STEREOS. SOMETHING *SAFE.*

I WANTED TO TALK TO *ROYAL.* I DON'T KNOW *WHY* -- HE'D JUST LAUGH AND CALL ME AN IDIOT, TELL ME TO *JUMP IN.*

GO ALONG TO *GET* ALONG, HE'D SAY. AND HE WASN'T THE *ONLY* ONE.

DARNICE? THESE BILLS -- THE NORDLING *CHARGE ACCOUNT* -- THEY'RE PRETTY HIGH, HONEY --

OH, THAT. MY NEW *COAT,* SOME SHOES. THAT *RED DRESS* YOU SAID I LOOKED SO GOOD IN. WE *GOT* THE CASH.

YEAH, BUT WE *AGREED* -- WE'RE PUTTING IT IN THE *HOUSE FUND.*

IF WE'RE CAREFUL *NOW,* WE CAN AFFORD A PLACE BY --

AWW, WE CAN PUT SOME *MORE* MONEY IN LATER...

HOW? WHERE'S IT GONNA *COME* FROM? WORKING EVEN *MORE* HOURS? OR WILL THAT JUST GO FOR *MORE SHOES?*

GOD, DARNICE, I'M RUN *RAGGED* AS IT IS -- AND THEN YOU WANT TO *GO OUT* ALL THE TIME.

WE GOTTA *SAVE,* BABE --

LANNIE SAYS --

I *AIN'T* LANNIE, OKAY? I *AIN'T* LANNIE!

SO I SAT AND *DRANK*, SPENDING MONEY LIKE WATER, HANGING OUT WITH LOSERS I DIDN'T EVEN *LIKE*.

TOO MANY NIGHTS THE *SAME*. NOWHERE WORTH GOING, NOTHING WORTH GOING *HOME* FOR.

NOT LIKE IT *USED* TO BE, WITH CHARLES. BUT WE HADN'T GOT PAST THAT *THING* THAT TIME.

'NOTHER *HERE*, PEEJ.

AND THAT GOLDDIGGER *WIFE* OF HIS, SHE DIDN'T LIKE ME. I SAW *THROUGH* HER, SHE DIDN'T WANT HIM SEEIN' *ANYTHING*.

SO I SAT AND DRANK, WISHIN' SOMETHING WOULD *HAPPEN*.

WISHIN' *NOTHING* WOULD.

HEY! IT'S *HIM*! IT'S TH' *STREET ANGEL*!

HUH?

ICE HIM!

JUST *LOOK* AT IT. AIN'T IT ALWAYS THE *WAY?*

WHUD KRAK

KLUDD KLOW

SOME WAYS, IT WAS LIKE WATCHING THE *OLYMPICS* ON TV, OLGA KORBUT AN' THAT. OTHER WAYS, *DIFFERENT.*

I REMEMBER WHEN STREET ANGEL FIRST *STARTED OUT,* BACK IN THE LATE SIXTIES. ALL THE TIME *SMILIN',* MAKIN' WITH THE BAD JOKES --

AH-AH!

PURSE-SNATCHING *AUTHORIZATION CHECK!* DO YOU HAVE A *LICENSE* TO DO THAT, SIR?

AND THE *HALOS.* HARD RUBBER HALOS THAT'D *STUN* YOU, ADHESIVE HALOS, SONIC HALOS -- EVEN BIG *CONSTRICTING* HALOS, SHRINK DOWN AND PIN YOUR ARMS TO YOUR SIDES.

RAKKT

NOT ANY *MORE.*

BY NOW --

THUK THUK THUK THUK

-- HE WAS *ALL BUSINESS.* NO MORE JOKES.

BUT THEN --

RUKK

THKK

K-KK

WHD

-- MAYBE HE DIDN'T SEE ANYTHING *FUNNY* IN IT ANY MORE.

HIGH-IMPACT *CERAMICS,* OVER A STEEL CORE. A *STEEL CORE.*

ALL RIGHT.

AT LEAST *FOUR* OF YOU KNOW SOMETHING ABOUT THE MORTELLARO KIDNAPPING. WHOEVER TALKS *FIRST* KEEPS THEIR *TEETH.*

WHO'S IT *GONNA BE?*

I SAW *LEFTY CARSON* SLIPPING OUT, LIKE HE WAS MORE THAN JUST HIS *USUAL* SCARED.

EXIT

WE DIDN'T KNOW WHAT *CHANGED* HIM, NOT THEN. WE'D JUST BEEN SEEING IT *HAPPEN,* MORE AND MORE IN RECENT MONTHS.

MAYBE IT WAS *NOTHING --*

-- BUT WHAT DID I HAVE *BETTER* TO DO? WAIT FOR HIM TO THINK MAYBE I KNEW ANYTHING ABOUT SUZZIE MORTELLARO?

SHE'S NOT WITH HIM SHE'S NOT WITH HIM MAYBE SHE'S GONE MAYBE SHE LEFT

OO.

B-BLACK VELVET...

YOU *KNOW.*

THE KNOWLEDGE OF THE MORTELLARO WOMAN ROILS OFF YOU LIKE *SWEAT.* TELL US WHERE SHE -- *WAIT.*

BLACK VELVET. STREET ANGEL'S *PARTNER,* THOSE DAYS. SHE'D SHOWN UP JUST BEFORE HE STARTED TO GET *REAL MEAN.*

NNH --?

ROYAL. IT'S *PETE.* SHAKE IT OFF AND GET UP. WE'RE ALL BEING *CALLED IN.*

THE NEXT *MORNING* --

BROUGHT YOU SOME *COFFEE,* CHARLES. MILK, ONE *SUGAR,* RIGHT?

HUH?

LANNIE NEVER BROUGHT ME *COFFEE* BEFORE. *SENT* ME FOR IT, NEVER BROUGHT IT. I DIDN'T KNOW WHAT WAS GOING ON.

BUT I DIDN'T THINK I *LIKED* IT.

YOU SEE? YOU *SEE?!*

BRAINTRUST! THAT FREAKIN', *MOTHERLESS* CANDIDATE FOR THE *PSYCHO HATCH!* HE THINKS WE TOOK HIS *WIFE*, AND --

NOBODY DOES THAT TO ONE OF MY CLUBS! I DON'T CARE *HOW* MANY HEADS HE HAS!

IT'S *WAR*, BOYS!

WAR!

IT WAS ANOTHER DAY FULL OF LANNIE'S LITTLE *STOPS*. THE ONES LANNIE GOT DARNICE ALL *WOUND UP* ABOUT.

ROYAL. OVER *HERE* A MINUTE.

HUH?

YOU LIKE TO HANG AROUND THE *EDGES*. OUT OF HARM'S WAY, OUT OF ANYONE'S *NOTICE*. THAT'S NOT GOING TO *WORK* ANY MORE.

DONNIE --

NO. WE'RE IN A WAR. NO MORE *HIDING* --

HEY, CHARLES. GET OUT OF THE *CAR* A SEC.

THE BOYS AND I HAVE BEEN *TALKING* ABOUT YOU. THIS WHOLE "I DON'T WANNA KNOW" THING. THAT'S NOT *GOOD* ENOUGH.

LANNIE, I WON'T --

NO. YOU *DO* KNOW. SO NO IN OR OUT --

JANUARY 19, 1977.

IF YOU WERE LIVING IN ASTRO CITY -- OR ABOUT *ANYWHERE* IN THE U.S. -- ODDS ARE YOU *REMEMBER* THAT DAY.

WRAK

BAK

KAKK

BUT NOT BECAUSE ME AND *SOME OTHER GUYS* FROM THE PLATYPUS MOB AMBUSHED A COUPLE OF *GUNBIRDS.*

AN' THAT'S *IT.* LOTTA HELP *YOU* WERE, ROYAL.

BLAM

AH -- I DON'T -- DIDN'T THINK YOU *NEEDED* --

NO, IF YOU REMEMBER *THAT DAY...*

WHAT THE *HELL* IS -- ?

the OUT-OF-TOWNERS

...IT'S BECAUSE IT'S THE DAY *HE* SHOWED UP.

HE WAS CALLED *THE INCARNATE,* BUT WE DIDN'T KNOW THAT, NOT BACK THEN. WE DIDN'T KNOW *ANYTHING.*

HE DIDN'T RESPOND TO *BULLHORN HAILS.* POLICE CHOPPERS COULDN'T GET *NEAR* HIM.

E.A.G.L.E. TROOPS TOOK OVER, CORDONING OFF THE AREA FOR DAYS. THE *FIRST FAMILY* CAME DOWN FROM ORBIT TO CHECK IT OUT.

THEY WEREN'T ABLE TO FIND OUT ANYTHING *EITHER.*

NATURALLY, THE *FRINGE ELEMENT* CAME OUT IN FORCE, LOOKING FOR SOME KINDA COSMIC *ENLIGHTENMENT.*

THEY TALKED ABOUT *"LEVELS OF PERCEPTION"* A LOT, BUT I DON'T THINK *THEY* GOT ANYTHING EITHER.

TAKE ME WITH YOU

THE REST OF US, WE WALKED ON *EGGSHELLS* THE FIRST FEW DAYS. MAYBE PRAYED A LITTLE MORE.

BUT IN THE END...

IN THE END WE DID WHAT WE *ALWAYS* DID, IN ASTRO CITY.

WE SHRUGGED, NICKNAMED HIM *"BIG JOE,"* AND WENT ON WITH THINGS.

HA!

OW! HEY!

BIG COSMIC *WHATSIT* IN THE SKY? YEAH, I HEARD. IT TALKIN' YET? *KILLIN'* ANYONE? NO? THEN LEAVE IT TO THE BIG BOYS, I GOT *THINGS* TO DO.

WE *GOOD,* ROYAL?

YEAH. I'LL GIVE JOE YOUR *BEST.*

FOR ME, THAT MEANT THE *GANG WAR,* CLICKIN' RIGHT ALONG.

I WAS WORKING ONE OF JOE THE PLATYPUS'S *CASINOS* WHEN BRAINTRUST SENT THE *DOMINOS* IN TO HIT US. BUT --

AWRIGHT, YOU LOWLIFE *SPOT-HEADS,* TIME TO -- -- HEY, YOU *ROBBIN'* THE PLACE?

WHAT?

OH, SH--

NOT *NO* MORE!

HELLHOUND WAS BACK IN TOWN.

WORD WAS, HE'D GOTTEN IN THE WAY OF A *GUN DEAL* OUT WEST, AND THEY'D PISSED HIM OFF. OR ELSE IT WAS ABOUT A *GIRL.*

EITHER WAY, HE HAD IT *IN* FOR BRAINTRUST, AND WASN'T BEING *GENTLE* ABOUT IT. WHICH WAS FINE BY ME.

HE MESSED UP *BRAINTRUST,* MAYBE THAT'D GET HIM OFF OUR BACKS. AND THEN WE'D HAVE TIME TO DEAL WITH *TOMMY GUNN* AND THE *DEUCE.*

BESIDES, HE WAS THE ONE WHO WAS ALL *BULLETPROOF* AN' HAD *DEMONIC STRENGTH* AND ALL. ME, ALL I HAD WAS A *GUN...*

...A HUGE UGLY CANNON I WAS SCARED TO EVEN *LOAD.*

YEAH, WHAT'RE *YOU* LOOKIN' AT, JOE?

156

NO. NOT *YOU.*

I SMELL A FILM OF *CORRUPTION* AROUND YOU, AND THE TAINT OF DARKNESS. BUT YOU ARE NOT ONE OF THEM.

NOT ONE I SEEK *REVENGE* ON -- NOR ONE I HUNT FOR *OTHER* REASONS.

STILL, I FEEL ONE OF THEM *NEARBY.* ONE OF THOSE WHO *VIOLATED* ME, WHO STOLE MY LIGHT, MY *SELF.*

SOMEWHERE. SOMEWHERE *NEAR...*

WHEN I WAS AT THE *PRECINCT HOUSE,* I SPENT A LOT OF MY TIME IN THE RECORDS ROOM.

AND NOT JUST BECAUSE I DIDN'T WANT TO *DEAL* WITH ANYONE.

ACPD File #...HH37FB/C
...ors / Organized Crime
...as Aloysius Gunn
...mmy" Gunn
...922

Once a soldier in the...
crime family, "Tommy" Gun...
to the vacu... created in t...
the Blue... created in t...
the Forgi... ...wings o...
the remain...
a smaller b...
Gunn lost th...
tle with the...
rebuilt by...
as a mechani...
fingers of wh...
capable of a...
fire, along...
attachment...
Gunn v...
powered en...
with trad...
structure...
his "Gun...

ACPD File #1968HH443TM/CC
Known Malefactors / Organized Crime
Subject: Brian Thaddeus Rusk
Aliases: Braintrust
DOB: 11/2/1931

History: A genius inventor cri... by po...
Rusk was victimized by busine... terests,...
notably Clement Technologies... who marketed...
discoveries but refused to p... him ...
profit shares. Incen... ...
robotic body and ha... ...
it, attacking and ki... ...
wronged him. He sal... ...
hooking them up to... ...
arrangement... ...
"comm... ...

ACPD File #1975MM393HM/CF
Known Malefactors / Organized Crime
Subject: Kuo Tseh-Shi
Aliases: "Bamboo"
DOB: 1/1/1951 (disputed)

History: The daughter of the internation...
Lord Talon (see EAGLE FILE 1WJJ2524GLM),...
(hereafter "Bamboo," I'm not going to kee...
slanty jibber-jabber - Mike) came to the...
the early 1970s, seeking to extend her fa...
centered criminal empire to the West. Cl...
In-The-Box, the Silver Agent, Hellhound...
however, and an apparent romance the Bla...
into conflict with her father, and event...
with his forces, a situation that still...
Her operations, centered in the Fujitani Ba...
built primarily on the heroin trade, but have encompassed other...
...trafficking, weapons trading, white slavery, blackmail and mind-control...
...often aimed at seizing control of city leaders, national...
...one occasion the entire U.N...
...through skilled martial artists, often unarmed,...
...nal Chinese and Japanese weapons, as...
...is an expert chemist, as...
...ellen, reptile ven...

ACPD File #1964HH37FB/C
Known Malefactors / Organized Cr...
Subject: Josef Andros Platapopou...
Aliases: The Platypus, Platypus...
...the Platypus, Joey Platypus
DOB: 6/29/1937

History: Born with physical a...
...that made him deformed and ugl...
Platapopoulous had an early li...
...buse and humiliation. ...
...The Platypus" at a...
...ed to have hi...
...him by na...

RECORDS
ROOM

MOST OF THE UNIFORMS
DIDN'T BOTHER *KEEPING
UP* ON THE FILES -- THEY
GOT THEIR INFORMATION
FROM THE *STREET.*

BUT IT WAS
PRETTY
INTERESTING.

BRAINTRUST IN *CITY
CENTER,* TOMMY GUNN
IN THE OLD *FORGIONE*
TERRITORY, BAMBOO IN
FUJITANI BAY...

Spend...
...in the Aus...
...Outback, Platy...
claims to have had...
visions that gave h...
...and mystic in...
...there is little o...
...his accent comes and goe...

ACPD File #1973HM322PM/VB
Known Superhuman / Vigilante
Subject: Rachelle H. Brown
Aliases: "Energy" Brown
DOB: 12/25/1955

History: A Bakerville prostitute, Br
fell under the thumb of Morris "The A
Reynolds (see ACPD File 1944HH12BCL/4
in his domination of the Negro mob
was seeking super-powered advantage

EAGLE File 1WPA8871BVU
** BULLETIN ** ACTIVE SUPERHUMAN *
Unaligned Superhuman / Vigilante
Codename: Hellhound
Real Name: M/Sgt. Harvard Amos Ch
DOB: 5/12/1947

Summary Overview: Whether the su
demonically enhanced, or w
conventional exp

EAGLE File 1WPP14667ABVS
** BULLETIN ** ACTIVE SUPERHUMAN ** BULLETIN
Unaligned Superhuman / Vigilante / Traveling
Codename: Black Velvet
Real Name: Unknown
DOB: Unknown

Primary Overview: Little is known of the su
prior to her becoming the superhuman known
Velvet. She is thought to have been a Harl
prostitute, captured among a group of inner
underclass subjects kidnapped nationwide in
used as subjects in the experiments of Dr.
Croft (crossref EAGLE file 1WMG1223CSG). N
been recovered on those experiments, but an
hearsay testimony indicates that they were
mutational experiments aimed at developing
powered enforcers for underworld figures in
late "Ace" Reynolds of Astro City, Damon B
Angeles and Oswald "Massacre" Morton of De
experimental subjects were killed, whether
experiments were successful or unsuccessfu
aim was to pioneer techniques that could b
male volunteers. A few subjects escaped,
including the subject codenamed Black Velv

Accreted testimony and data indicates
subject was put through painful and invas
experimentation designed to affect physic
metaphysical systems including her limbic
Kirlian systems. Note: The Kirlian
recognized by the AMA, but
criminal scient

.E File 1WPM5456VTBR
ULLETIN ** ACTIVE SUPERHUMAN
ve Superheroes / Vigilantes/
Name: The Jade Dragons
Name: (s) Gary Samuel Nov
Shimasa Takamura
(in both cases) - 8/17/1958

ry Overview: Novak and Taka
gs, children of the Japane
Takamura, aka the Dragon
File 1WMT3333FCL), born at
to different mothers. Ac
the Dragon Shogun's pow
ed by his eldest child wh
appears that, when Takamu
Yakuza ganglords, his
the two children, allow
he full measure of it o

ware of each other

THEY'D PRETTY MUCH STUCK TO
THEIR *OWN* AREAS, UNTIL THEY
GOT STIRRED UP. SOME GOT *HIT*,
MAKING THE OTHERS GREEDY...

MOSTLY, IT
WAS *MASKS*
DOING THE
STIRRING UP.

LIKE *THESE*
GUYS.

TWIN CHILDREN OF DIFFERENT
MOTHERS, HOWEVER *THAT*
WORKS. THEIR *SUPER-
GANGSTER* DAD GETS
KILLED, THEY EACH INHERIT
HALF HIS *POWER* --

ptive father why he h
and it caused much strife betwe

however, she has named herself Black Velvet.
punish those who kidnapped her and aided in Croft's expe
her, which left her skin chalk white and
her soul damaged or missing.
France, Italy, Mor

-- AND *BAM*, THEY'RE OUT FOR REVENGE.

STOLEN SOULS, DEAD *RELATIVES*, HEROIN-TRADE *JUNKIE SISTERS* -- THEY WERE ALL MAD ABOUT *SOMETHING*, AND OUT FOR BLOOD.

I DON'T MUCH LIKE THE MASKS THAT WERE AROUND *BEFORE* THEM --

-- BUT AT LEAST *THEY* MOSTLY SEEMED TO WANT TO *HELP* PEOPLE.

WILLIAMS. HEY, *WILLIAMS* --

AND THEN THERE WAS THE *OTHER* REASON I HUNG OUT IN THE RECORDS ROOM.

I *DIDN'T* WANT TO DEAL WITH ANYONE. NOT LANNIE, NOT HIS FRIENDS, AND *ESPECIALLY* NOT THAT INTERNAL AFFAIRS WEASEL *SAAF*.

GOT A *MINUTE*, WILLIAMS?

NOT REALLY. I GOTTA GET *HOME.*

YOU CAN GIVE ME *NAMES*, WILLIAMS. NAMES, TIMES, *AMOUNTS.*

I CAN PULL YOU IN *OFFICIALLY*, IN FRONT OF THE WHOLE *SQUAD!*

HAVE A *CRAPPY* DAY, SAAF.

I DIDN'T WANT TO *KNOW*. I'D *TOLD* THEM I DIDN'T WANT TO KNOW. NOT ABOUT THE PAYOFFS, THE FAVORS, *NOTHING*.

BUT THEY DIDN'T FEEL SAFE UNLESS I WAS *IN*.

AND OF COURSE, WHEN I *TURN DOWN* THE PAYOFF THEY FORCE ON ME TO MAKE ME ONE OF THEM, LANNIE TELLS *DARNICE*.

KLEK

SHE CALLS ME AN IDIOT. AND *LEAVES*.

-- MASSIVE FIGURE ASTRO CITIZENS CALL *"BIG JOE."* IT SEEMS JOE MAY BE GROWING A *BRAINSTEM*, AND A NERVOUS SYSTEM --

AND I HAVE TO *WONDER* --

-- HOW SAFE DO THEY FEEL *NOW?*

I HAVE *TOUCHED* YOU. TOUCHED YOUR *HEART* WITH MY DARKNESS.

I SHOULD *NOT* KILL YOU. YOU ARE ONE OF THEM, ONE OF THOSE WHO *DID* THIS TO ME. I SHOULD *NOT* KILL YOU, BUT I WISH --

N-NO! PLEASE -- P-*PLEASE* DON'T --

FLEE.

FLEE BACK TO YOUR *MASTERS.* AND TELL THEM I HUNT *THEM,* TOO.

OHMIGOD. OHMIGOD. I'M *ALIVE* --

TELL THEM YOU HAVE LED ME *TO* THEM --

AIN'T MUCH FOR *CHIT-CHAT*, ARE YOU, DEKE? I DON'T LIKE A GUY DON'T *TALK* MUCH. IT'S LIKE HE'S *HIDIN'* SOMETHING.

MY *APOLOGIES*, THEN. I DON'T SEE MUCH *USE* FOR IDLE TALK.

BUT I'LL *WORK* AT IT.

HNH.

WELL, IT'S AN *INTERESTIN'* PROPOSITION, I'LL TELL YOU THAT MUCH. I'LL THINK IT *OVER*, GET BACK TO YOU.

I CAN ASK *NO MORE*, SIR. NOW, IF YOU'LL *EXCUSE* ME...?

SURE, SURE. GIVE MY BEST TO *JOE*, HUH?

WITH ALL DUE RESPECT, MR. GUNN, I DON'T THINK I'LL *DO* THAT. NOT AT *THIS* JUNCTURE.

HA! NO, I GUESS YOU *WON'T*, EH?

I GUESS YOU *WON'T*.

HEH.

I'D DONE **GOOD,** FOR ONCE. BUT IT DIDN'T MAKE ME FEEL **PROUD.** JUST -- NOTICEABLE.

AND BEING NOTICED ISN'T ALWAYS SUCH A **GOOD THING.**

THIS GUY. THIS **GUY!** YOU **SEE** THIS GUY?

DOWN UNDER Club

UNDER ATTACK FROM THE DOMINOS -- **AND** THAT DAMNED HELLHOUND -- AND DOES HE JUST RUN? **NO!** HE **SAVES** THE NIGHT'S TAKE! AND HE GOT WHAT THOSE SPOTHEADS LOOTED FROM THE **CUSTOMERS,** TOO!

THE DOMINOS'LL THINK THE **POLICE** GOT THE LOOT, THE COPS'LL FIGURE ONE OF THE **DOMS** GOT AWAY WITH IT...

HA! I BEEN **HEARIN'** ABOUT YOU, WILLIAMS -- THAT YOU HANG BACK, YOU HIDE. BUT THIS -- THIS IS **SMART THINKIN'!**

A STRONG MAN NEEDS **SMART THINKERS** AROUND HIM, KIDDO. AND **LOYAL** ONES. AIN'T THAT **RIGHT,** DEKE?

OF **COURSE,** SIR.

I JUST -- I SAW THE **BAG,** AND KNEW EVERYONE WAS PANICKING, SO --

IF YOU'LL PARDON THE **INTERRUPTION,** SIR --

-- YOUR DELIVERY FROM **CHICAGO** IS HERE.

-- AND THEY'RE WHO HE WENT TO FOR HELP WITH THE *OTHER GANGS.*

KZZT

KZZT

SORRY ABOUT THAT, MR. P. JITTERJACK GETS A LITTLE... *FRISKY* WHEN HE'S BEEN CONFINED TOO LONG. UNDER CONTROL *NOW,* THOUGH.

THE *BOYS* SHOULD HAVE BEEN FASTER ON THE DRAW WITH THE STUN-STICKS. *APOLOGIZE,* BOYS.

SORRY.

UH, YEAH --

THE GUY INTRODUCED HIMSELF -- *AUBREY JASON,* A TIGER-LEVEL *PYRAMID* OFFICER.

BUT THE WAY HE SMILED -- THAT WAS NO *MISTAKE,* KILLING RICKY. HE WAS LETTING THE BOSS KNOW WHO WAS IN *CHARGE* HERE.

AND THERE WAS SOMETHING *ABOUT* HIM, SOMETHING I COULDN'T PUT MY *FINGER* ON RIGHT AWAY --

BOSS! *BOSS!*

OUTSIDE -- YOU GOTTA *SEE* --

WE *FELT* IT THEN, IN OUR HEADS. AND WE REALIZED WE'D BEEN FEELING IT *ALL ALONG.*

BUT IT WAS *FEATHER-LIGHT* BEFORE, AND NOW --

IT WAS PRESSURE, *HEAT* -- AND THERE WAS SOMETHING *BEHIND* IT, SOMEONE --

-- LIKE BEFORE, WE'D JUST BEEN BEING *WATCHED,* BUT NOW -- IT WAS *HUNTING* NOW, WHATEVER IT WAS. AND IT HAD ANSWERS --

-- ANSWERS IT DIDN'T *LIKE* --

EGRON BECOMES NARMAD...

THE SIFTER FADES. THE JUDGE RISES...

HUH?

WE DIDN'T KNOW IT THEN, BUT THAT *MENTAL CONTACT,* IT WAS BEING FELT ALL OVER THE COUNTRY, OVER MOST OF THE *WORLD.*

E.A.G.L.E. COMMANDER! PLEASE *ADVISE!* SUBJECT IS --

AND ALL OF A SUDDEN, WE FELT IT *CHANGE.* THAT COLD DISAPPROVAL KINDA *RIPPLED* -- AND IT WAS LIKE IT WENT FROM BEING ONE PERSON TO *MORE* --

-- FROM ANGER TO CONFUSION, THEN TO CONCERN, TO *DETERMINATION* --

AND THAT *GLOWERING FACE,* IT LOOKED -- LIKE IT HAD TO BELCH --

AND THAT WAS THE SCENE AT *GAVIN WERNER SQUARE* THIS AFTERNOON, AS THE *APOLLO ELEVEN* MADE A DARING ESCAPE.

TO *DISCUSS* THOSE EVENTS -- AND THE BIZARRE MANIFESTATION THAT *PRECEDED* THEM --

-- WE HAVE WITH US IN THE STUDIO *SIMON MAGUS*, OCCULTIST, REPUTED *SORCERER*, AND *POLICE CONSULTANT* ON A FEW NOTABLE CASES, THESE PAST FEW YEARS.

WELCOME, SIR.

THANK YOU, JANE.

AS WE SAW ON THE TAPE, APOLLO ELEVEN'S *LEADER,* JOHN GARRISON, SAID *"TOO SOON,"* AND *"WASN'T TIME."* IS THIS *SIGNIFICANT?*

VERY *MUCH* SO. BUT TODAY -- IT'S ONLY THE TIP OF THE *ICEBERG.*

THE *BEING* WE SAW -- THAT THE ELEVEN EITHER SUMMONED OR BANISHED -- IS KNOWN AS THE *INCARNATE.*

IT IS AN EMISSARY OF A *GALACTIC CIVILIZATION,* SENT EITHER TO OFFER NEW CULTURES MEMBERSHIP, OR *ELIMINATE* THREATS.

IT LIKELY JUDGED US A *THREAT.*

IT -- WAS GOING TO *ELIMINATE* US?

PFF, NO NEED TO *DWELL* ON IT.

BUT THERE ARE *OTHER* COSMIC SIGNIFIERS AT PLAY.

SOMETHING ELSE IS COMING, A THING OF *GREAT POWER.* I CAN'T SEE IT *CLEARLY* YET -- STILL, IT *SHOULD* NOT BE RELATED TO ANY OF THIS.

AND YET, IT *IS.* AND WE MUST DEAL WITH IT *CAUTIOUSLY...*

-- HEARD IT HERE *FIRST,* FOLKS: TODAY'S EVENTS MAY BE *ONLY* THE BEGINNING.

OF COURSE, HE HADN'T *SAID* THEY WERE THE BEGINNING, HAD HE? JUST THAT THINGS WEREN'T *OVER.*

THE BEGINNING -- WHO KNOWS *WHEN* THAT WAS? WHATEVER IT WAS, IT MIGHT HAVE BEEN A LONG TIME COMING.

AND IT MIGHT HAVE STARTED A LOT *SMALLER* THAN ANY FOO-FOO MAGICIAN WHO LIKES TO BE ON TV WOULD'VE *NOTICED...*

WILLIAMS.

I TOLD YOU *ALREADY,* SAAF. I DON'T HAVE ANYTHING TO *SAY* TO YOU.

SURE YOU DO.

THE THING IS, WILLIAMS, YOU'VE GOT A *CHOICE.* YOU CAN HELP BRING IT DOWN, OR YOU CAN GO DOWN *WITH* IT.

OUT. *OUT!*

SCARED, WILLIAMS? OF WHAT?

INTERNAL AFFAIRS? DON'T NEED TO BE SCARED OF US UNLESS YOU'VE DONE SOMETHING *WRONG.* OR IS IT YOUR FRIENDS? IF THEY *ARE* YOUR FRIENDS.

MY DOOR'S ALWAYS *OPEN,* WILLIAMS...

THEY *WEREN'T* MY FRIENDS. THEY NEVER *WERE.*

BUT *YEAH*, I WAS SCARED.

-- ON THE *HOUSE*, YOU HEAR ME? ROYAL HERE, HE DON'T PAY FOR HIS DRINKS *NO MORE!*

I'M GIVING YOU A *CREW*, KID. FAST THINKER LIKE YOU, I NEED YOU DOIN' MORE THAN JUST LIFTIN' AND *CARRYING*, GET ME? I LIKE LOYALTY, AND I *REWARD* IT.

YOU REPORT DIRECT TO *ME*, OR TO *DEKE.*

UH, THANKS...

I GOT MY *EYE* ON YOU, KID! I GOT MY *EYE* ON YOU!

MAN, TOMMY GUNN'S NOT GONNA KNOW WHAT *HIT* 'IM. AND CHICAGO -- I'M GETTIN' THE *HEAVY HITTERS*, I'M GETTIN' *RESPECT* --

I WAS SCARED, TOO. BUT IT WAS *MORE* THAN JUST THAT. I DIDN'T *WANT* TO BE NOTICED, DIDN'T WANT TO MOVE UP. BUT --

THERE WAS *SOMETHING ELSE* GOIN' ON. THE GUY FROM CHICAGO. AUBREY JASON. SOMETHING *ABOUT* HIM --

BOSS SEEMS PRETTY *HAPPY* WITH YOU, HM? LOOKS LIKE YOU'RE *GOING* PLACES.

NOT *ME*, NO. I'M JUST -- I WAS *LUCKY*, THAT'S ALL...

OH, I DON'T KNOW. DON'T SELL LUCK *SHORT*, FRIEND. EVERYONE STARTS *SOMEWHERE*, AFTER ALL.

TAKE *ME*, FOR INSTANCE.

I WASN'T MUCH OLDER THAN YOU WHEN I GOT *MY* FIRST SQUAD.

JUST *JACKAL-LEVEL*, BUT I WAS IN COMMAND. AND IT WASN'T EASY -- BUT I ROLLED WITH THE PUNCHES AND *LEARNED*, AND HERE I AM.

NO, DON'T SELL LUCK *SHORT*, ROYAL...

AND THEN I HAD IT. I KNEW WHAT WAS *BUGGING* ME ABOUT HIM.

I ALWAYS *SAID* I'D NEVER FORGET THAT FACE. THAT *SCAR*.

THE *FACE* OF THE MAN WHO'D *KILLED OUR PARENTS*...

Television

ATTEND ME.

I READ THAT *BOOK* SHE WROTE, IN THE MID-EIGHTIES, AFTER THAT BUSINESS WHEN MAGUS *DISAPPEARED.*

IT SAID *SHE* WAS THE REAL POWER, AND HE JUST CHANNELED IT. ALL THE BIG OLD SPELL-BOOKS WRITTEN BY *MEN,* THAT KIND OF THING.

I AM *HERE,* MASTER.

AND MAYBE SHE WAS *RIGHT,* OR JUST TAKING THE CREDIT ONCE HE WASN'T THERE TO ARGUE, I DON'T KNOW.

YOU ARE *WOMAN.* THE WELLSPRING, THE BEARER, THE *SOURCE* OF *ALL LIFE.*

I AM *MAN.* THE STAFF, THE *MIND,* THE SHAPER OF WISDOM. *OPEN* TO ME.

OPEN TO ME.

SHE'S DONE PRETTY WELL ON HER *OWN,* THOUGH, EVER SINCE. SO MAYBE THERE'S SOMETHING TO IT. DOESN'T *MATTER,* I GUESS.

HE WAS THERE, AND WAS GOING TO BE *MORE* THERE. THAT'S WHAT MATTERED, RIGHT THEN.

HEY, LOOKS LIKE WE ATTRACTED A LITTLE *HELP!*

DIVE IN, FRIEND. *PLENTY* TO GO AROUND.

HELLHOUND, *NO!* WATCH YOURSELF, THAT'S --

≡GHKK!≡

HOUND DOG.

HOUND DOG.

PUPPY DOG.

OOH. CLOWN.

WRAKRAKRAK

THKASSH
THKASSH

CLOWNIE *CLOWN* CLOWN. HNN. *SHADOW* MANS.

OHHHHHH....

SORRY, TRIED TO *TELL* YOU. THAT'S *JITTERJACK.* HE'S TOUGHER THAN HE LOOKS, AND DEFINITELY *NOT* ON OUR SIDE.

HE *KILLED* 'EM. *ALL* OF 'EM.

BUT HE'S WORKING FOR *PLATYPUS JOE,* EVERYONE KNOWS THAT. THE DEUCE WAS SPARRING WITH *BAMBOO.* WHY WOULD...?

I SMELLED *BLOOD* ON HIM ALREADY, TOO. THINK MAYBE HE'D ALREADY FOUND WHERE YOU LEFT *BAMBOO'S* GUYS?

LITTERING THE STREETS WITH FREAKIN' *NINJAS.* OUGHTTA BE A LAW...

YOU COULD FEEL IT IN THE *AIR.* THIS WAS GOING TO BE BAD. THING WAS, THOUGH, I *DIDN'T CARE.*

IT WAS ALL TOO MUCH. MY *WIFE* DITCHING ME. MY PARTNER TRYING TO PULL ME INTO THE *SEWER* WITH HIM AND HIS BUDDIES.

INTERNAL AFFAIRS TRYING TO GET AT MY PARTNER THROUGH ME.

I DIDN'T CARE ABOUT *ANYTHING* ANY MORE.

I WENT OUT ON A *DATE.* I FELT LIKE I SHOULD, WITH DARNICE GONE. AND CHARLENE IN DISPATCH, SHE'D *SMILED* AT ME A LOT.

WELL, THAT WAS NICE.

NO, IT WASN'T. WHAT'RE YOU *TALKING* ABOUT?

YOU DIDN'T SAY *TWO WORDS* IN THERE, WILLIAMS. NOT *TWO WORDS*. YOU MIGHT AS WELL HAVE BEEN *ALONE!*

MAYBE YOU'RE NOT OVER YOUR *WIFE* OR WHATEVER. THAT'S COOL. BUT THEY *GOT* TVS IN THERE, YOU DON'T *NEED* A DATE.

THANKS FOR THE *PIZZA*.

I SHOULD HAVE FELT BAD. SHE WASN'T *WRONG*. BUT I JUST COULDN'T BRING MYSELF TO CARE.

NOT ABOUT *DINNER*, NOT ABOUT LANNIE OR THE RAT SQUAD, NOT ABOUT DARNICE, NOT ABOUT *ANYTHING*.

DOWN UNDER Club

I DON'T *GET* IT.

WHADDYA *MEAN*, HE KILLED 'EM *BOTH*?

I WISHED I COULD TALK TO CHARLES.

WE ALREADY *HAD* THEM AT EACH OTHER'S *THROATS!* HE WAS JUST SUPPOSED TO KILL THE *DAMN* NINJAS --

-- MAKE BAMBOO THINK THE *DEUCE* DID IT, GET HER SO MAD SHE WOULDN'T BE *LOOKIN'* OUR WAY! BUT IF THEY'RE *ALL* DEAD --

I WAS GETTIN' IN DEEPER AND DEEPER WITH THE *PLATYPUS*, WHO HAD A *PSYCHO KILLER* RUNNING AROUND --

-- NOT TO MENTION THE *PYRAMID SKELL* THAT KILLED OUR PARENTS --

WELL, JITTERJACK *CAN* GET A LITTLE EXCITED --

A *LITTLE*--!

CALM YOURSELF, SIR...

PERHAPS THIS CAN WORK TO OUR *ADVANTAGE.* IF THEY DON'T *KNOW* IT WAS US, THEY'LL SIMPLY LASH OUT AT OTHER TARGETS --

BACK NOW. *BACK* NOW. *TREATS?*

AND THERE WAS *SOMETHING ELSE* GOIN' ON, SOMETHING I DIDN'T HAVE FIGURED YET. I WISHED I COULD TALK TO *CHARLES.*

BUT EVEN IF WE'D BEEN *SPEAKIN'* TO EACH OTHER, BACK THEN, THERE WOULDN'T HAVE BEEN *TIME* --

-- SHOCKING *BULLETIN,* WITH NEW INFORMATION *JUST NOW* COMING IN!

POLICE HAVE RECOVERED A *BODY* FROM THE WATERS OF LAKE MICHIGAN, NEAR THE MILWAUKEE WATERFRONT --

-- A BODY *CONCLUSIVELY IDENTIFIED* BY DENTAL RECORDS AS NOTED CRIMINAL SCIENTIST *DR. LEWIS OSCAR CROFT!*

MORE, ACCORDING TO *TAPED CONVERSATIONS* SEIZED IN RAIDS ON THE HEAD-QUARTERS OF DETROIT CRIMELORD "MASSACRE" MORTON --

-- RECENTLY CAPTURED BY LOCAL VIGILANTE *MISTER BADD* --

-- THE DEATH WAS A *CONTRACT KILLING.* A CONTRACT KILLING IN WHICH THE KILLER WAS NONE OTHER THAN *BLACK VELVET* --

-- THE *MYSTERIOUS,* SHADOW-CLOAKED CRIMEFIGHTER WHO HAS OF LATE BEEN A PARTNER TO *ASTRO CITY'S* OWN *STREET ANGEL!*

CROFT, IMPLICATED IN THE CREATION OF *NUMEROUS* SUPER-BEINGS, HEROES *AND* VILLAINS -- INCLUDING BLACK VELVET, *"ENERGY" BROWN* AND THE *THUMPER* --

-- WAS MISSING AND *THOUGHT DEAD* LATE LAST YEAR, IN THE WAKE OF A BATTLE THAT DESTROYED HIDDEN *WAREHOUSE LABS* --

-- BUT THE *INCRIMINATING TAPES*, ALONG WITH INDICATIONS THAT THE BODY WAS *DELIBERATELY HIDDEN*, HAVE LED POLICE TO ISSUE A WARRANT FOR --

ORDINARILY, I THINK WE'D HAVE *SHRUGGED IT OFF.*

A *MAD SCIENTIST,* GOING UP IN FLAMES WITH HIS OWN PLANS? IT'S NOT LIKE IT'S UNUSUAL -- EVEN WHEN THEY *DON'T* COME BACK.

EVEN THE *MURDER.* THE MASKS GOT ACCUSED *ALL THE TIME,* AND IT USUALLY TURNED OUT TO BE A *FRAME.* BUT THIS TIME --

BLACK VELVET HAD NEVER REALLY *FELT* LIKE A HERO, NOT TO MOST.

AND WITH THE *GANG WAR,* AND WITH VELVET BEING STREET ANGEL'S *PARTNER,* AND HIM GETTING HARDER, MORE *VICIOUS* --

WE *REMEMBERED* THE BLUE KNIGHT. AND WE LOOKED AROUND, AT *HELLHOUND,* THE ANGEL, THE *JADE DRAGONS,* MISTER BADD, OTHERS --

AND WE WONDERED HOW MUCH *DIFFERENCE* THERE WAS BETWEEN THE "GOOD GUYS" AND THE CROOKS ANY MORE.

CHARLES.

LANNIE. WE NEED TO TALK.

NO, WE DON'T.

BUT --

I DON'T CARE.

WE'RE PARTNERS, WILLIAMS --

YEAH? SHOVE YOUR --

CODE ONE!

EVERYBODY HIT THE BRICKS! YOU'RE OFF-DUTY, YOU'RE ON DINNER BREAK -- YOU'RE BACK ON!

WARRANTS CAME THROUGH -- ON BLACK VELVET AND STREET ANGEL. AND MORE --

"-- WE GOT A SIGHTING!"

:PFF!: YOU'RE TAKING **ME** IN. AND HOW HAVE **I** TRANSGRESSED AGAINST YOUR CODE?

WE **BOTH** DO JUSTICE, **OUTSIDE** THE LAW.

I DON'T **KILL.**

OH?

HOW MANY HAVE YOU LEFT LYING IN **ALLEYWAYS** THESE PAST TWO YEARS, SKULL FRACTURED, **LUNG** PUNCTURED? HOW MANY **INTERNAL INJURIES?**

DID THEY ALL GET **MEDICAL ATTENTION?** DID THEY ALL **LIVE?**

DID THEY?

I -- I NEVER -- I HADN'T **THOUGHT** -- DID **YOU** --

LORD IN HEAVEN ABOVE, I'VE **SEEN YOU** TAKE A MAN'S SOUL AND TURN IT **INSIDE OUT.** DID YOU **DO** THIS TO ME? DID YOU **MAKE** ME INTO -- ?

OH, YOU'D LIKE TO **THINK** SO, WOULDN'T YOU?

THAT YOU WERE **PURE** AND **FINE,** WITHOUT REPROACH -- UNTIL THE EVIL **SHADOW-WITCH** CORRUPTED YOU. THAT IT **CAN'T** BE YOUR FAULT.

DID YOU EVER THINK MAYBE -- **YOU JUST LIKED IT?**

NO WAY WE COULD *KEEP UP* WITH THEM, OF COURSE. BUT WE RADIOED IN WHICH WAY THEY WERE GOING.

DISPATCH TOLD US TO STAY ON THE *CLOCK* --

-- SAID IT FELT LIKE IT WAS GOING TO BE A *BIG NIGHT,* LIKE SOMETHING WAS GOING TO *BREAK.*

FELT THAT WAY TO *ME,* TOO.

CHARLES!

I *SAID* WE GOTTA *TALK.* WE'RE *PARTNERS,* MAN -- YOU DON'T JUST SHUT ME OUT LIKE --

IS *THAT* HOW IT WORKS? I LOOK OUT FOR *YOU, YOU* LOOK OUT FOR YOU, TOO? THAT'S *PARTNERS?*

HEY, NOW --

I DON'T WANT *ANY PART* OF IT, LANNIE. I DON'T WANT TO *TALK* TO YOU, TO *SAAF* IN I.A.D., TO *ANYONE!*

I DIDN'T WANT ANY PART OF WHAT YOU WERE DOING FROM THE *START.* I *STILL* DON'T! YOU GOT A PROBLEM? I *DON'T CARE!*

SO *YOU,* SAAF, YOUR BUDDIES -- *DO WHATEVER THE HELL YOU WANT,* LANNIE!

JUST *LEAVE ME OUT OF IT!*

TOP STORIES *TONIGHT* --

-- IN THE WAKE OF SHOCKING ALLEGATIONS ABOUT *BLACK VELVET,* E.A.G.L.E. TECHNICIANS MAY NOW HAVE LINKED HER TO A *SERIES OF KILLINGS,* IN NEW YORK, L.A., CHICAGO --

-- AND ARE SCANNING THE VICTIMS OF *UNSOLVED MURDERS* FOR TRACES OF HER DISTINCTIVE *SHADOW-ENERGY* --

-- THE *APOLLO ELEVEN* ARE CAUGHT ON TAPE IN A CONFRONTATION AT THE U.N. --

...WANT TO DO IS *TALK,* EXPLAIN WHAT *HAPPENED!*

WE'RE NOT HERE TO *HARM* ANYONE! JUST TO OFFER PEACE, *TECHNOLOGY* -- A PLACE FOR *HUMANITY* IN THE STARS! THE *STARS!* ARE YOU ALL *INSANE?!*

-- AND THE *FIRST FAMILY* RETURN FROM THEIR *INTER-DIMENSIONAL GOODWILL TOUR!*

THEIR CONFERENCE WITH THE PRESIDENT AND HIS TOP ADVISORS HAD TO BE *DELAYED,* HOWEVER, AS WITHIN HOURS OF THEIR RETURN THEY WERE *OFF AGAIN* --

IT WAS A *CRAZY* NIGHT.

BLACK VELVET WAS ON HER *KILLING SPREE*, HITTIN' PEOPLE IN HALF THE MOBS IN TOWN -- WITH THE *ANGEL* ON HER HEELS ALL THE WAY.

THE BOSSES FIGURED NOW WAS THE PERFECT TIME TO STRIKE AT WHOEVER THEY WERE *MAD* AT, WHILE THEY WERE RATTLED.

NO! NO KILLING!

TROUBLE IS, THEY WERE *ALL* RATTLED. AND EVERYBODY TRIED TO HIT *EVERYONE ELSE.*

AND SOME PEOPLE WERE *LOOTIN',* OF COURSE -- GET PEOPLE WORKED UP, MAKE 'EM THINK THINGS ARE FALLING APART, OR THE *LAW* AIN'T THERE --

-- IT DOESN'T TAKE MUCH TO MAKE 'EM JUST THINK ABOUT *NOW,* NOT TOMORROW.

AND IT DIDN'T SEEM LIKE IT WAS EVER GONNA *END* --

YOU. *"SCARS" GORHAM.*

YOU HELD THE *KNIFE* TO MY THROAT, WHILE YOUR FRIENDS INJECTED THE SEDATIVE. I WANTED *YOU* TO KNOW IT WAS COMING.

FRAKKK

VELVET, *STOP* THIS! YOU CAN'T --

THREE *MORE,* THEN MY *EMPLOYER.*

FOR THOUGH I HAVE USED MY ROLE AS HIS *ASSASSIN* TO GET CONTACTS AND INFORMATION I NEEDED, HE *IS* AN EVIL MAN --

197

-- AND HE *CANNOT* BE ALLOWED TO *PROFIT* FROM THIS NIGHT!

...CANNOT BE ALLOWED TO *PROFIT* FROM THIS NIGHT!

MMM. *THAT* WON'T DO. THAT WON'T DO *AT ALL.*

AH, MR. *MACMANUS?*

WHO...?

AHH, MR. WILLIAMS. YOUNG MR. WILLIAMS. COME IN, COME IN, MAKE YOURSELF WELCOME. AND IT'S *"DEKE,"* YOU KNOW THAT.

NOW, HOW CAN I *HELP* YOU, MY FRIEND?

AH, WELL -- I WAS WONDERING -- YOU HANDLE A LOT OF THE COMMUNICATION WITH JOE'S *"ASSOCIATES"* IN OTHER CITIES --

-- AND I FIGURE YOU COULD USE, Y'KNOW, *EYES* AND *EARS* THERE.

AND ASTRO CITY -- I DON'T THINK IT'S FOR *ME,* NOT ANY MORE. IT'S JUST TOO *CRAZY* AROUND HERE.

SO IF I WAS TO HEAD TO, SAY, LOS ANGELES, *SAN FRANCISCO* --

-- WOULD YOU PUT IN A *WORD* FOR ME? GET ME IN WITH *JOHNNY DARK?* OR THE *BIRDMAN?*

WELL NOW.

I *HAD* MARKED YOU OUT AS A SMART ONE, HADN'T I?

AND HERE YOU ARE, *PROVING* IT. BUT LET ME MAKE YOU A *COUNTEROFFER*, MY FRIEND.

WAIT, SAY, *TWO WEEKS*. IF YOU STILL WANT TO GO, I'LL GET YOU THE PLACE OF YOUR *CHOICE*.

AH...

IN THE MEANTIME, THOUGH -- *YES*, IT'S CHAOTIC. BUT RIDE IT OUT, RIDE IT OUT. HAVE A DRINK. *BIG THINGS* ARE COMING.

I THINK YOU'LL FIND THAT WHEN IT'S ALL OVER, THINGS *WILL* SETTLE DOWN --

-- SETTLE DOWN QUITE *NICELY* --

I DIDN'T *BELIEVE* HIM.

THINGS MIGHT SETTLE DOWN NICE FOR *HIM*, THAT I COULD BELIEVE. BUT FOR ME?

DOWN UNDER Club

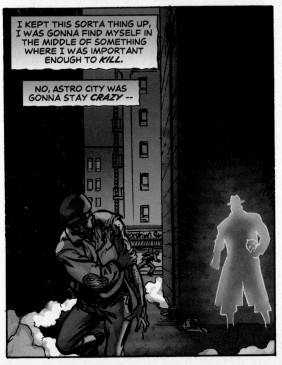

I KEPT THIS SORTA THING UP, I WAS GONNA FIND MYSELF IN THE MIDDLE OF SOMETHING WHERE I WAS IMPORTANT ENOUGH TO *KILL*.

NO, ASTRO CITY WAS GONNA STAY *CRAZY* --

I'M *HERE!* THEN THERE'S NO TIME TO *LOSE* --

-- AND I WAS GONNA *GET OUT.* AND THE ONLY REGRET I HAD --

THAT ONE NIGHT, BACK IN 1977 -- THAT WAS MAYBE THE *SINGLE WORST NIGHT* OF MY LIFE.

AND I'M *NOT* TALKING ABOUT WHAT WAS GOING DOWN IN THE REST OF THE CITY. THAT STUFF, THAT WAS *PRETTY BAD*, THOUGH.

STAPLES! CARBON PAPER! PENCILS! CUTTING BOARD! YAAAAH!

YAAAAAAHH!

OKAY....

WHAT *SET IT OFF* --

OKAY, YOU REMEMBER. BLACK VELVET WAS ON HER *KILLING SPREE*, TAKING OUT EVERYONE WHO'D HELPED MAKE HER WHAT SHE *WAS*.

SHE WAS PLANNING TO *FINISH UP* WITH THE MOBSTER SHE'D BEEN *WORKING* FOR. AN' THE *STREET ANGEL* WAS AFTER HER, TRYING TO BRING HER IN.

:HLPHHH!:

HE DIDN'T *FIND* HER. *JITTERJACK* DID.

WHITE-BLACK GIRL. *SHADYLADY.*

DARK INSIDE. DARK DARK *DARK.*

JITTERJACK WAS WORKING FOR THE *PLATYPUS*, BORROWED FROM *PYRAMID* IN CHICAGO. AT LEAST, WE *THOUGHT* HE WAS.

BUT PALE *OUTSIDE.* LIKE JITTERJACK, A LITTLE. YOU TWO PARTS, JITTERJACK TWO *PIECES.*

I SEE THAT. WHAT DO YOU *WANT?*

CALM-TALKING MAN, AND *MAN-WITH-TREATS.* THEY SAY YOU *BAD*, NOT DO WHAT YOU TOLD.

THEY SAY *KILL YOU*, BRING BACK *HEART.*

GET *TREATS.*

HO! WORMIES!

MACMANUS? YOU'RE WORKING FOR *DEKE MACMANUS*?

TELL HIM HE DIES LAST -- BUT HE DIES *TONIGHT*! TELL HIM I'M *COMING FOR HIM*!

KRATT

NO. NO TREATS FOR *THAT*.

STRONG WORMIES!

HE *WILL*! HE'LL *DIE*! HE'LL *DIE LIKE THE REST*!

YOU *LIKE* THIS, DIVIDED MAN? YOU'RE *MINE* NOW, LIKE THE OTHERS.

N-NO... DON'T LIKE WORMIES...

MY POWER FLOWS *THROUGH* YOU. MY DARKNESS TOUCHES YOUR *HEART*. TOUCHES IT, *SQUEEZES* IT...

...*CLENCHES* IT UNTIL IT STILLS. HOW DO YOU LIKE *THAT*, MADMAN?

NOT... NOT *GOOD*. HEART... BREAKS.

B-BUT...IS GOOD THING FOR J-JITTERJACK...

...HE HAVE SPARE!

NO

DIDN'T GET THEM ALL YET

BUT I WAS TELLIN' YOU ABOUT *ME*. AND *MY* BAD NIGHT --

ROYAL!

ROYAL!

UH, RIGHT *HERE*, SIR. WHAT --?

IT'S ALL DOWN THE *CRAPPER*, ROYAL.

FIREFIGHT'S *SIX BLOCKS* AWAY, AND GETTIN' *CLOSER*. NO GOIN' TO GROUND THIS TIME. I'M WRIGGLIN' *OUT OF HERE*.

GET UP TO THE *GUN CACHE*. YOU KNOW THE ONE. THIS'LL DEACTIVATE THE FAILSAFES, GET YOU IN THE *EMERGENCY HATCH*.

WARM UP THE *TUNNELER*. I'LL BE *TWENTY MINUTES* BEHIND YOU. IT'LL BE YOU, ME, AN' *DEKE*. OFF TO CANBERRA, AND *NEW PLANS*.

GO.

I *ALREADY* WANTED OUT -- THAT PART SOUNDED FINE. BUT *WITH* THE PLATYPUS? AND DEKE? I DIDN'T *KNOW* ABOUT THAT.

I THOUGHT -- THOUGHT WE'D BE ABLE TO *TAKE ADVANTAGE* OF THE CHAOS, HIT THE DEUCE AND BRAINTRUST, TAKE A LITTLE *GROUND*.

BUT THERE'S *ANOTHER PLAYER*, SOMEONE WHO WAS READY FOR *ALL* OF US. SOMEONE INSIDE -- SOMEONE IN THE *THICK* OF IT --

TURNED OUT *THAT* WASN'T WHAT I NEEDED TO WORRY ABOUT.

SIR.

DEKE! WHAT'S GOING ON? WHO'S *DOING* THIS? IF I ONLY KNEW WHO THE BASTARD *WAS,* I'D --

PERHAPS A LITTLE *LOGICAL CONSIDERATION.* THE ANSWER WOULD SEEM TO BE *REASONABLY* CLEAR.

IT CANNOT BE ONE OF THE *EXISTING CRIMELORDS.* FROM REPORTS, *EVERYONE* IS BEING HIT --

-- AND THE DAMAGE DONE IS *TOO GREAT* TO BE A SHAM. OUR MYSTERY ACTOR IS DESTABILIZING *EVERYONE.*

RIGHT, *RIGHT...*

IT IS NOT AN *OUTSIDER,* EITHER. WHOEVER IT IS, HE KNOWS A *GREAT DEAL,* INFORMATION THAT COULD ONLY COME FROM *INSIDE.*

AND *YEARS* INSIDE, AT THAT. THIS IS A *LIEUTENANT,* SOMEONE MAKING A BID FOR *DOMINATING POWER* AT A SINGLE STROKE.

BUT -- MOST OF *THEM* ARE DEAD, TOO --

AND LASTLY, IT MUST BE SOMEONE WITH THE *BACKING* TO TAKE CONTROL, AMID ALL THE CHAOS. SOMEONE WITH *CONTACTS.*

A LONG WORKING RELATIONSHIP WITH *PYRAMID,* PERHAPS.

WHAT? BUT THAT WOULD --

NO, DEKE.

NO, *NO...*

MM.

AUBREY?

IS IT **DONE,** THEN?

YES. TELL THE OTHERS TO **MOVE IN** NOW. WE HAVE **FIVE HOURS,** I EXPECT, BUT I ESTIMATE WE'LL CONTROL **80%** OF THE CITY'S UNDERWORLD BY DAWN.

I THINK I'LL BE CALLING MYSELF *THE DEACON.* SOME OF THE MEN *ALREADY* CALL ME THAT, BEHIND MY BACK. IT'S GOT *PRESENCE,* I THINK.

IT COMMANDS *RESPECT.*

HUFF

HUFF

HE'D SENT ME TO THE *GUN CACHE.* I'M SURE ALL HE MEANT WAS FOR ME TO GET HIS *ROBO-MOLE-MACHINE,* LIKE HE SAID.

WITH DEKE, IT MIGHT HAVE BEEN SOME SORT OF *MESSAGE* --

BUT NOT WITH THE *PLATYPUS*. DEVIOUS LIKE THAT JUST WASN'T HIS STYLE.

I *KNEW* ABOUT THE GUN CACHE, OF COURSE. I'D KNOWN WE MAINTAINED AN OFFSITE STORAGE AND TRANSFER POINT FOR *YEARS*.

EARLY ON, I'D EVEN SOLD THE LOCATION TO LANNIE FOR A LITTLE EXTRA *BEER MONEY*.

WH -- WH --

CHARLES!

CHARLES! WHAT HAP -- ARE YOU -- *CHARLES* --

HH

I'D *SOLD* IT TO HIM, AND WHEN HE NEEDED A PLACE THAT'D THROW SUSPICION ON *OTHERS*, HE'D USED IT.

JUST BREATHE. JUST *KEEP BREATHIN'!* I'LL GET *HELP!*

OFFICER DOWN! ANYONE *THERE?* YOU GOT A OFFICER *DOWN!* HE NEEDS AN *AMBU--*

D-DON'T -- WONT WORK --

THERE WAS JUST *SO MUCH* GOIN' ON...

THERE'S *TROUBLE* IN THE CITY.

WHAT? *C'MON!* CAN'T I WASH OFF SOME A' THIS *DEMON BLOOD* FIRST?

STOW IT, JULIE. THIS IS IMPORTANT.

THAT CORONA OF DARK ENERGY -- THAT'S *BLACK VELVET.* THERE'S NO SIGN OF THE ENERGY-FLOW *DIMINISHING* --

-- AND IT'S MORE THAN ENOUGH TO ENGULF THE *ENTIRE CITY.* WE'VE GOT TO FIND SOME WAY TO --

HMM. *THAT'S* ODD. THAT PRESENCE -- THE *INCARNATE* -- IT'S STILL *THERE,* STILL HOVERING *NEAR* HER, AS IF IT'S OBSERVING --

SO WHAT DO WE *DO,* DAD?

I'M...NOT *SURE,* NICK. THE *CONTAINMENT FIELDS* WE'VE DEVELOPED -- THEY WON'T HOLD BACK *THAT* SPECTRUM OF POWER.

BUT MAYBE, JUST *MAYBE* --

FROM WHAT I'VE BEEN ABLE TO *GLEAN* ABOUT THIS WEAPON SINCE WE RECOVERED IT, IT COULD TEAR A HOLE IN *REALITY ITSELF.*

IF I *MODIFIED* IT, CHANNELED ITS ENERGY...

ARE YOU MAD?!

HM?

LOOKS LIKE *THAT'S* BEING HANDLED -- AS WELL AS IT'S *GOING* TO BE, AT ANY RATE. I'D BETTER --

I CAN *EASE* YOUR PAIN. TAKE IT *AWAY.* DO YOU WANT ME TO DO THAT?

W-WILL I...LIVE *THROUGH* IT?

I'M SORRY. THAT, I *CAN'T* DO.

G-GOOD.

BARBARA VANE. *BLACK VELVET.*

PLEASE... P-PLEASE...

YOU HAVE BEEN *WRONGED,* BARBARA VANE. AND NOW YOU WRONG *OTHERS.* IS THIS WHAT YOU *WANT?*

N-NO... I...I *DID,* B-BUT... S-SO MUCH *PAIN...*

DO IT, PLEASE. *NOW.*

VERY *WELL.*

FREEZE!

FREEZE, POLICE!

OH, THANK GOD.

IT'S MY *BROTHER* -- HE'S ONE OF YOU, HE'S A COP -- HE NEEDS *HELP* --

IT WASN'T ME -- IT WAS *BENT COPS*, LANNIE MCDONNELL AND HIS BOYS -- HE NEEDS AN *AMBULANCE*, A DOCTOR --

DROP THE WEAPON! HANDS IN THE AIR! NOW! *NOW!*

MY BROTHER...

AGAINST THE WALL! MOVE!

GOT HIM *CUFFED* -- HE WON'T BE ANY MORE TROUBLE --

HEY, HE MIGHT BE *RIGHT.* THIS IS CHARLES WILLIAMS. LOOKS LIKE FOUR-FIVE IN THE BACK. NOT ANY OF *THESE* WEAPONS, EITHER.

HE'S STILL ALIVE. I'VE GOT A *SIGNAL,* I'M CALLING IT IN...

OH, THANK *GOD...*

IT WAS THE *WORST* NIGHT OF MY *LIFE.* I WASN'T THINKIN' ABOUT THE OTHER STUFF, I DIDN'T *CARE* ABOUT THE OTHER STUFF...

I DON'T --

WHERE AM --

WHAT -- I WAS -- MY OFFICE --

IT ALL *FADED*, AS QUICK AS IT STARTED. LIKE WATER RUNNIN' OUT OF A TUB, OR SOMETHING. IT WAS *OVER*.

OR IT *SEEMED* LIKE IT, AT LEAST.

I'M SORRY FOR ALL THAT *HAPPENED* TO YOU, BARBARA. AND ALL YOU DID IN *RETURN*.

I HOPE YOU'RE AT *PEACE*.

AND *YOU*. YOU STILL HAVE A *CHANCE* TO TURN THINGS AROUND, FIND A BETTER WAY.

NO ONE COULD TELL ME IF YOU *DID* OR NOT, BUT...

EXCUSE ME. THIS MAN NEEDS ATTENTION. HE'S HEALING VERY *QUICKLY*, BUT --

THE *SILVER AGENT?*

THE *SILVER AGENT!* IT *IS* YOU!

TIME-TRAVEL! IT'S TIME-TRAVEL

YOU'RE GOING BACK TO '73

DON'T DO IT

DON'T GO BACK

ELECTRIC CHAIR

THEY KILL YOU

DON'T GO

THANKS, PEOPLE. I'M GLAD TO KNOW I MAKE IT ALL THE WAY BACK. THAT MEANS A LOT TO ME.

WOULD YOU GET A MESSAGE TO HONOR GUARD FOR ME?

HAVE THEM MEET ME BY THE FALLS, AT 10:33AM ON MAY 3, 1982. AND HANG IN THERE...

...IT DOES GET BETTER.

AND WITH THAT, HE VANISHED ONCE MORE, LEAVING A CITY TO PONDER THIS DAY, AND WHAT LIES AHEAD...

...AND TO BEGIN TO DIG OUT FROM THE SHATTERING ORDEAL.

THE BODY COUNT IS ONLY BEGINNING TO BE KNOWN. AND THE PRICE... WHO CAN EVEN GUESS AT IT?

THE CREATURE THAT WAS ONCE HELLHOUND HAS ESCAPED, AND NO ONE KNOWS WHERE TO. THE CONTROVERSIAL STREET ANGEL IS AMONG THE MISSING AS WELL.

THERE WAS A LOT TO TAKE IN, A LOT THAT GOT SHOOK UP. BUT THEY MISSED THE BIG ONE.

AND POLICE REPORT THE CAPTURE OR SURRENDER OF *DOZENS* OF ORGANIZED CRIME FIGURES...

YEAH, HELLHOUND TURNED UP BACK IN *VIET NAM,* AN' THE STREET ANGEL RAN MEDICINES INTO *CENTRAL* AFRICA FOR A WHILE.

BAMBOO LEFT THE U.S., BRAINTRUST WAS THOUGHT *DEAD,* THE DEUCE, TOMMY GUNN AND THE PLATYPUS *WERE* DEAD.

THEY SAW ALL THAT AN' THOUGHT *HOORAY,* THAT'S LESS TO BE SCARED OF. THEY DIDN'T SEE THE DEACON *AT ALL.* NOT *YET.*

THEY DIDN'T THINK ABOUT THE *INCARNATE,* AN' WHAT IT MIGHT BE *HERE* FOR.

BUT FAIR'S FAIR. I DIDN'T THINK ABOUT IT EITHER.

TWO MORE *MINUTES,* WILLIAMS. NOTHING MORE --

THEY BENT THE *RULES* A LITTLE. LET ME IN TO SEE HIM BEFORE TAKING ME DOWNTOWN TO *BOOK* ME.

FIGURED THAT WITH WHAT I'D DONE TO GET THEIR *ATTENTION,* I'D EARNED THE RIGHT TO SAY *GOODBYE.*

BUT I WASN'T *THERE* TO SAY GOODBYE. *HE* WAS READY FOR THAT. I WASN'T.

WE BARELY HAVE A *PULSE,* HIS HEARTBEAT IS IRREGULAR. OFFICERS, WE *REALLY NEED* TO --

JUST A COUPLE SECONDS OF *PRIVACY,* NURSE. PLEASE.

THEY'LL BE HERE TO TAKE HIM TO *SURGERY* IN A MINUTE. YOU'VE GOT *THAT.*

THANKS, I -- *THANKS.*

I BARELY *BREATHED* IT. I KNEW THAT COP ON THE DOOR WAS *LISTENING*.

I *SAW* HIM, CHARLES. I KNOW WHO HE *IS*. THE MAN WHO KILLED MA AND POPPA IS OUT THERE, WALKING AROUND, *SUCKING IN* AIR.

BUT I *KNOW WHO HE IS.*

I DIDN'T KNOW IF HE EVEN *HEARD* ME.

C'MON, WILLIAMS. TIME TO *GO*.

HE DIDN'T MOVE, DIDN'T SO MUCH AS *TWITCH*.

I DON'T KNOW IF HE EVEN *HEARD* ME...

DOCTOR. DOCTOR, HIS *HEARTBEAT'S* STRONGER. HIS PULSE ISN'T AS *THREADY*...

I *HEARD* HIM. I HEARD HIM *JUST FINE.*

END OF BOOK TWO

SKETCH
BOOK
**DARK
DESIGNS**

A vast, decades-spanning saga with dozen of superheroes in it? Always an enjoyable challenge, particularly when all of the heroes will be period pieces, and need to feel like they belong to their particular era.

The Black Badge, for instance. He'd been mentioned before, and seen as an old man -- but to tell a story set in Bakerville in the late 1950s, we needed to see him in his prime, at a time the only outright black superhero in American comic books may have been Lion Man, from All-Negro Comics #1 (and only). He had to have the simplicity of Fifties hero design, feel pre-Silver Age (so he should feel as much like a detective hero as a superhero), look like a character who could have turned up in at least a tryout backup tale or two, and still be cool.

lose skull cap

Lando Calrissian

dashing adventurer.

Badge-shaped tunic

ARMORED SHIELD REMOVABLE FROM CHEST

PRINTED PATTERN REMAINS ON CHEST

"BLACK BADGE" 1958

12-10-03

Previous page: Initial designs for our leads, Charles and Royal Williams.

THE BLACK BADGE THE BLACK BAD

BRASS SHIELD

It took a few tries, but Brent and Alex nailed it, I think.

wavy "Lando" hair

Domino mask

Pencil thin mustache

Badge shield removable from chest

jodpurs

Alex Raymond boots

"BLACK BADGE 12-17-03

And then it's the 1970s, and we need Seventies heroes, from a troubled biker Vietnam vet-turned-monster (see our cover gallery for sketches of Hellhound), to a no-nonsense street hero (more in the mode of Cleopatra Jones and Coffy than John Shaft, for a change), and kung-fu heroes.

"Energy" Brown became our bad-neighborhood street hero -- or at least one of them.

And Dragonclaw, here, became the basis for the Jade Dragons, who melded kung-fu crime adventure with a little hint of Shazzan.

"Energy Brown"
ACDAZ #1
9-9-06

A string tie with either outline of Australia

Bush hat?

a Platypus or a Kangaroo

webbing

Hands large— webbing semi-flyer 3 fingers

ACDA2 #1

Joey 'The Platypus' Platapopulous 9-9-06

Saf w/t

"The EXPERIMENTALS" ACDA BOOK I #4 8-20-05 (1½ hrs) (1 hr)

What's a good gangwar without grotesque crimelords? Joey "The Platypus" Platapopoulous fills the bill in fine style. Along with Braintrust, Tommy Gunn, Bamboo and more, but who's counting?

The Experimentals, mentioned in an early story but seen for the first time here, are actually late Sixties heroes, but their career spills over into the Seventies and beyond, so it was time to design them. Here they are: Solid, Liquid, Vapor, Ener-Jeannie and their fifth member, so mysterious even they don't know about him. Or her. Or it. They'll be

SIMON MAGUS

Alternate medallions

"SIMON MAGUS"
AC:DA #2
3-18-05
(4 hrs)

"GRIMOIRE"
ACDA #2
4-13-05

- Add fringe
- rings on toes + fingers

"GRIMOIRE"
in Haïk ACDA #2
4-28-05

SIMON MAGUS

HAIR WHITE IS LUMINOUS, CASTING FACE INTO PERMANENT SHADOW. EYEGLASSES ARE LIT GREEN.

LACED SHIRT AND HIGH-COLLAR VEST ARE OPTIONS.

LEFT BREAST PINNED CLOAK COULD ADD MAJESTY.

WALKING CANE/SWORD

REMOVED FROM CANE/SCABBARD

SYMBOL/MEDALLION IS A STYLIZED OWL FACE MADE FROM HALF A PENTAGRAM.

FOIL-STYLE SWORD

← 3½" WIDE

MEDALLION ON TOP CAN BE SEEN THROUGH IRON RELIEF.

Simon Magus took some work as well, as our first attempts at a timeless sorcerer who combined Edwardian mannerisms and John Lennon granny glasses kept coming off as old rather than timeless, or fussy rather then enigmatic. Alex transformed him into something the felt like counterculture wisdom drawn from timeless traditions.

And Grimoire, Simon's "assistant" -- Brent realized her beautifully. A female character whose power is given lip service while the men have all the fun. Even the enlightened had some more enlightening to do. But the Eighties are coming like a freight train...

GURU

OLLO ELEVEN THE APOLLO ELEVEN

lex's name, so he got to bear the brunt of designing eleven superheroes who looked like a 1970s team, looked appropriately alien, and could play the part of the cosmic peace-ambassadors-from-space who seem to spend all their time fighting. A wonderful collection of alien archetypes, assembled around one Earth-hero icon as leader.

GAS GIANT

SHADOW AREAS ARE LUMINOUS HOT PINK

GOLD FACEPLATE

SHINY WET RED SKIN

STAR PILOT

WHITE SUIT W/ RED BANDS

RED THE NAVIGATOR

MERCURY RED

GAS GIANT
JUNO, JUPITER

THE OUTLAW

Mercury Red, The Outlaw and Guru were possibilities as Seventies heroes who didn't get to turn up. Will the future hold a role for them? You never know.

APOLLO 11

LITTLE STARS OUTSIDE OF BLACK BODY MEMBERS

GRAY SKIN

ALMOST A PLASTIC MAN TYPE

WALKING BLACK HOLE

YELLOW GLOW ON HEAD

COMET HEAD

SILVER BODYSUIT

FISH GUY

GREEN TEAL SHINY SHELL EXTERIOR.

YELLOW EYES

COVER GALLERY

ARMAMENT
SPECIFIC
TO EACH
INDIVIDUAL

- FACE PLATES
- BRACELETS
- NECKLACES
- WRISTLETS
- GAUNTLETS
- CIRCUITRY
- HOLSTERS
  & STRAPS
- BREATHING OR
  FUEL TANKS
- HOSES

FOR
60's
JUST
GUNS
NO TRIANGLE
SKIRTS
866.

"PYRAMID AGENTS"
(70's version)
12-24-'98

DARKNESS FALLS

OF WAR CASUALTIES OF WAR CASUA

ON DAY EXECUTION DAY EXECUTION DAY EXECUTIO

COVER DESIGN IS NEW ANGLED GRAPHIC FOR ALL "BOOK TWO" STORYLINES

ASTRO CITY THE DARK AGE BOOK TWO

BLACK VELVET

SHE HAS ONE DEVIATION IN THE OUTFIT, WHERE HER SUNGLASSES HAVE HIGHLIGHTS STANDING OUT FROM THE REST OF THE BLACK.

BODYSUIT IS A PURE BLACK LIKE HANOK'S COSTUME, WITH NO HIGHLIGHT DETAILS.

IMAGES OF FIGURES ARE MONOCHROMATIC INDIGO PAINTINGS WHILE LOGO FRAME AND WALL BELOW THEM ARE MAGENTA COLOR HOLDS.
I'M GOING FOR A MORE POP ART GRAPHIC.

THE ONLY COLOR ON BLACK VELVET APART FROM HER FLESH IS THE SATIN FINISH MAGENTA INSIDE HER CLOAK.

DRAPERY IS NOT TOO LONG, OR DOWN TO THE GROUND.

GAS
GIANT

STAR
PILOT

RED

HELLHOUND

6'5"

BROWN SKIN — SKIN MAY BE
A FINE COAT OF FUR

BLACK LEATHER

Thanks to the usual suspects — Lawrence
Watt-Evans, Karl Kesel, Richard Howell,
James Fry and others — for tirelessly
serving as sounding boards. Thanks also
to my mother, for sharing her perspective
on the 1960s and 1970s.
— KURT BUSIEK

I thank the City of New York, which was
in the throes of The Dark Age when
I first arrived there in 1976, for its
immeasurable inspiration in the object
creation of Astro City.
— BRENT ERIC ANDERSON

My thanks to Marcus McLaurin for
allowing Kurt and me a home for our
Marvels project so many years ago and
driving both of us elsewhere to elaborate
upon its inspiration for Astro City. Also
thanks to Bob Schreck, formerly of Dark
Horse Comics, whose embrace of the
Dark Age concept and dismissal of the
previously-agreed upon Astro City series
would cause us to realize the importance
of building up that universe first before
fulfilling this project.
— ALEX ROSS

ACKNOWLEDGMENTS